Ethnic Knitting
Exploration

MW00377739

Ethnic Knitting
Exploration

Lithuania, Iceland,
and Ireland

by Donna Druchunas

NOMAD PRESS FORT COLLINS, COLORADO

Dedication

For Deb, who believes in my ideas and makes them real.

The cover sweaters are described on pages 143 (upper sweater) and 53 (lower sweater).

Interior design by Deborah Robson

Interior image processing by Rebekah Robson-May

Copyediting, proofreading, and index by Kathryn Banks, Eagle-Eye Indexing

ISBN 978-0-9668289-9-3

Printed in the United States of America

Nomad Press
PO Box 484
Fort Collins CO 80522–0484

www.nomad-press.com

10 9 8 7 6 5 4 3 2 1

Books by Donna Druchunas

Ethnic Knitting Exploration *
Ethnic Knitting Discovery *
Arctic Lace *
Kitty Knits
The Knitted Rug

* Published by Nomad Press.

Author websites:

www.sheeptoshawl.com

www.ethnicknitting.com

This book is an introduction to a few of the many knitting traditions from around the world. It contains texture and color patterns from different regions and provides instructions for designing and knitting sweaters with different shapes and specific construction techniques. It is prepared with appreciation for the knitters who have come before us.

Ethnic Knitting Discovery—Drop-shoulder sweaters, with and without half-gussets and steeks, from the Netherlands, Denmark, Norway, and The Andes.

Ethnic Knitting Exploration—Raglan, circular-yoke, and saddle-shoulder sweaters inspired by the traditions of Lithuania, Iceland, and Ireland, with additional instructions for modifying any sweater from pullover to cardigan.

Nomad Press contributes a percentage of its resources to non-profit organizations working on projects related to the topics of its books.

Nomad Press is a proud member of and participates in the Green Press Initiative, which  works to create paper-use transformations that conserve natural resources and preserve endangered resources.

Library of Congress Cataloging-in-Publication Data

Druchunas, Donna.
  Ethnic knitting exploration : Lithuania, Iceland, and Ireland / by Donna Druchunas.
    p. cm.
  Includes bibliographical references and index.
  ISBN 978-0-9668289-9-3 (pbk. : alk. paper)
  ISBN-10: 0-9668289-3-3 (alk. paper)
  1. Knitting—Lithuania—Patterns. 2. Knitting—Ireland—Patterns. 3. Knitting—Iceland—Patterns. I. Title.
TT819.L57D79 2008
746.43'2—dc22
                              2008037728

Contents

Introduction

I love traditional textiles and clothing. Although I do sometimes buy a sweater made in the current fashion, most of the sweaters in my closet were made by my grandmother in the middle of the twentieth century. They are classic designs that never go out of style. My grandmother knitted from patterns, but in earlier times around the world knitters made sweaters without patterns, using stitch designs and sweater-shaping techniques passed down to them from their own grandmothers.

The sweaters and projects in this book are all inspired by traditional ethnic garments knitted using old-fashioned techniques from different parts of the world. While differing in details, ethnic knits share a few common traits. Most are knitted in the round using double-pointed and circular needles. They are knitted without line-by-line instructions or written patterns. Each item is a unique combination of pattern stitches and colors, made using traditional knitting techniques. The stitch patterns are passed on to new knitters by families and friends.

Some traditional sweaters were made as straight tubes with little or no shaping. These drop-shoulder and square-armhole designs are easy to knit and design, but because they have no shoulder shaping they do not provide a flattering fit for all figure types.

Ethnic Knitting Exploration introduces three sweater shapes that are more tailored to fit the shoulders than

In the knitting instructions

 Capital letters (**A**) in dark symbols stand for **measurements**.

Lowercase letters (**a**) in lighter symbols stand for **stitch counts**.

the early drop-shoulder and square-armhole alternatives: the raglan, the yoke, and the saddle-shoulder. Each of these styles takes a different approach to shaping and each is used with different types of color and texture patterns. One chapter here also provides instructions for making any sweater into a cardigan.

Chapter 1 describes the sweater shapes that are included in *Ethnic Knitting Exploration*. If you are unfamiliar with raglan, yoke, or saddle-shoulder construction, start here for a quick overview.

Chapter 2 provides instructions for a few basic skills. If you're a curious knitter, skim this chapter in advance. Otherwise refer here when you need help with one of the techniques used in the projects.

Chapters 3 through 5 feature knitting techniques and designs from Iceland, Lithuania, and Ireland.

Each of these chapters includes:

✓ A small **practice project** such as fingerless gloves, a capelet, or a poncho

✓ **Visual sweater plans** for knitters who are ready to fill in the numbers and do the math on their own with a few clues

✓ **Sweater-planning worksheets** for knitters who like to plan their own projects and figure out all of the measurements and stitch counts in advance

✓ **Step-by-step project sheets** for those knitters who may need to be guided through the process the first few times

The final chapter provides instructions for knitting cardigans.

I hope the designs in this book inspire you to try knitting accessories and sweaters from around the world, using the construction techniques and pattern stitches that have been used traditionally in the three regions that we're exploring in these pages.

Sweater shapes
raglan, yoke, and saddle-shoulder

Sweaters come in almost as many shapes and sizes as people do. The simplest sweaters are straight tubes that surround the body with two smaller tubes attached to the shoulders for sleeves. I explained how to make these simple sweaters in *Ethnic Knitting Discovery*.

Refining the shoulder area

Other sweater shapes surround the body in a more form-fitted way, tapering above the armholes to drape more naturally around the neck and shoulders. Some of them allow sleeve patterns to run uninterrupted from the cuffs to the neckline.

In this book, I will present three common sweater shapes made with different yoke and shoulder-shaping techniques. Each of these designs flatters different figure types and, depending on the yarn weight and pattern stitches used, can be knitted to suit children, women, and men.

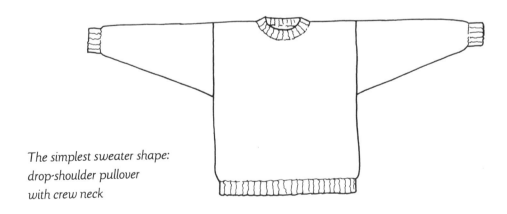

The simplest sweater shape: drop-shoulder pullover with crew neck

8

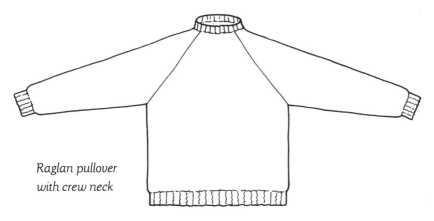

Raglan pullover with crew neck

Raglan sweaters

The raglan sweater is a modern design that has been popular since the 1960s. The body is knitted in the round to the armholes, then set aside. Each sleeve is then knitted in the round from the cuff to the underarm. Then all three pieces—body and two sleeves—are joined together on a large circular needle and worked in the round for the upper body.

Paired decreases shape the upper body and form shoulder "seams" that extend from the underarm to the neck. These aren't real seams; they just look like they might be. After the knitting is completed, the small openings at the underarms are grafted together. There are no other seams.

Yoke sweaters

The yoke sweater is similar to the raglan, but instead of decreasing at fixed points in the upper body, you spread the decreases across the yoke. This produces a smooth area without any appearance of seams between body and sleeves.

Although the total number of decreases worked in the upper body is the same as for a raglan, a yoke sweater contains fewer decrease rounds. For the yoke sweater, you work even for several inches, then decrease 25 percent of the stitches on a single round. You repeat this process two more times, decreasing 33 percent on the second decrease round and then 40 percent of the

The sweaters in this book feature refinements in the shoulder area.

9

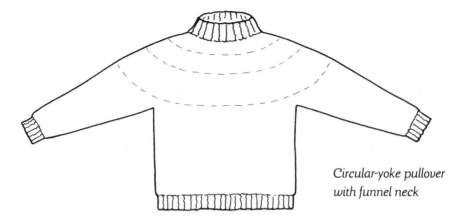

*Circular-yoke pullover
with funnel neck*

stitches on the third decrease round. After knitting the three yoke sections and decrease rows, you are ready to knit the neck.

Saddle-shoulder sweaters

The saddle-shoulder sweater is similar to the simple drop-shoulder sweater, except that a thin panel extends from the top of the sleeve to the neckline, separating the front and back shoulders. The addition of this thin panel, called a saddle, drops the back neckline and makes shaping of the front neck a cinch.

This type of sweater is most often knitted flat (instead of in the round) with intricate cable designs. I prefer to work these sweaters flat, but also provide tips on knitting saddle-shoulder sweaters in the round for advanced or adventurous knitters (see page 160–161).

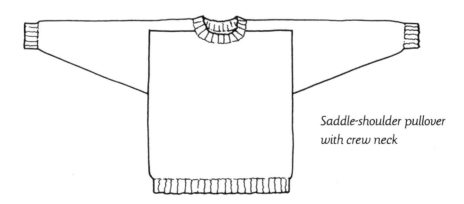

*Saddle-shoulder pullover
with crew neck*

Pullover or cardigan—you choose!

I will also explain how any basic sweater shape can be made as either a pullover or a cardigan. Cardigans can be made in several ways. You can knit a cardigan just as you would a pullover and then cut the fabric open at the front; or you can knit the sweater body back and forth, in one big piece, with the rows beginning and ending at the front opening; or the sweater can be knitted flat in pieces and sewn together. Pages 162 to 168, in the chapter on cardigans, describe these alternatives.

Sizing guidelines

Knitting a sweater that comes out the intended size is not difficult, but it doesn't happen without a little forethought.

First, you must know what size you plan to make. You can determine this by measuring another garment that is the right size, or by measuring the recipient and adjusting the body measurements for ease (ease is the extra fabric that keeps a sweater from fitting like a glove . . . unless you want it to).

Second, after you determine the required measurements for your sweater, you must knit a gauge swatch to make sure your knitting will come out the right dimensions. The following pages will walk you through the process of selecting a size and checking your gauge.

Selecting a size

The size charts on page 16, from the Craft Yarn Council of America's *Standards and Guidelines for Crochet and Knitting*, list the dimensions of basic sizes for children, women, and men. The accompanying drawing shows the relative proportions of sweaters knitted in different shapes.

Instead of working from a size chart, I prefer to measure my favorite sweater or sweatshirt and copy its dimensions, but the charts are very useful when I am designing sweaters for other people. Always calculate the dimensions of the sweater based on the finished measurements of the garment, not on the actual body measurements. Most of us don't want skin-tight sweaters. We prefer a bit of ease to make the sweater more comfortable and flattering. The amount of ease can vary depending on the type of fit you prefer.

Note: Most of the worksheet examples in this book are based on a 40-inch (102-cm) sweater and a gauge of 5 stitches to 1 inch (20 stitches to 10 cm). The gauges for the design samples shown in the project illustrations vary.

Getting gauge

After choosing a size, you must make sure that you can knit a sweater that matches your desired measurements. To consistently knit sweaters that fit the intended recipient, you must always knit a gauge swatch.

Using the same stitch pattern that you will use in your project and needles that are an appropriate size for the yarn you've chosen (see page 21), cast on about 20 to 24 stitches and work until you have about 5 inches (12.5 cm) of knitting. If your project will be knitted in the round, your swatch should also be knitted in the round. Many knitters find that they get a different gauge on the same stitch pattern when knitting circularly than they do when knitting back and forth.

How to measure gauge

Stitch gauge is important in almost all projects. If your stitch gauge is not exact, your sweater will not come out the right size. To measure the stitch gauge, place a ruler or tape measure across your swatch horizontally. Mark the beginning and end of 4 inches (10 cm) with pins and count the stitches between the pins. Divide by 4 to calculate the number of stitches per inch (if you are working in metric measurements, leave the number as is for the number of stitches in 10 cm).

Row gauge is also important in sweaters with yoke shaping. To make sure the yoke on your sweater comes out the correct width and depth, the decreases must be spaced properly and this is determined by row gauge. To measure the row gauge, place a ruler or tape measure across your swatch vertically. Mark the beginning and end of 4 inches (10 cm) with pins and count the rows between the pins. Divide by 4 to calculate the number of rows per inch (again, leave the number as is for the number of stitches in 10 cm).

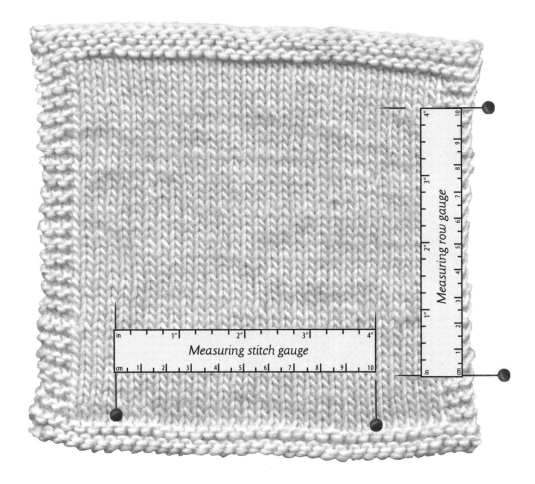

Measuring stitch gauge

Measuring row gauge

Simple sweater proportions
— raglan & yoke

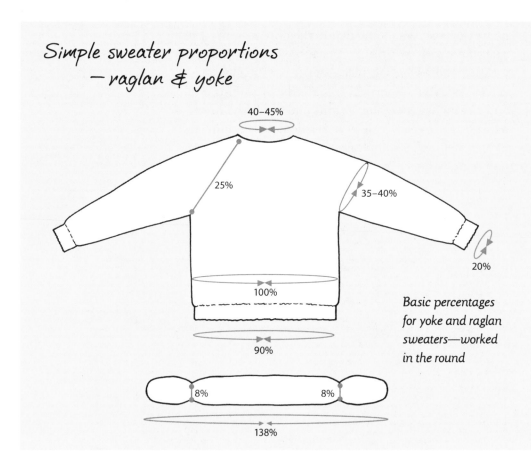

Basic percentages for yoke and raglan sweaters—worked in the round

Tips for raglan & yoke shaping

You may have noticed that on both the raglan and the yoke sweater, the depth of the yoke equals approximately ½ of the body width, or ¼ of the body circumference. In reality, the yoke of a sweater is almost never more than 11 or 12 inches (28 or 30.5 cm) long, and in some cases you may need to fudge on the yoke depth to make a sweater that actually fits.

When you are knitting for someone who is very tall or very thin, you may find that you need to lengthen the yoke. Conversely, when you are knitting for someone who is short or robust, you may need to shorten the yoke.

This can be accomplished quite easily by spacing out the decrease rounds in a different sequence than the one specified for an average sweater.

To lengthen the yoke, on a raglan work two plain rounds between decrease rounds, or on a yoke sweater work several extra plain rounds before each decrease round.

To shorten the yoke, on a raglan alternate between working decreases every round and every other round, or on a yoke sweater work fewer plain rounds before each decrease round.

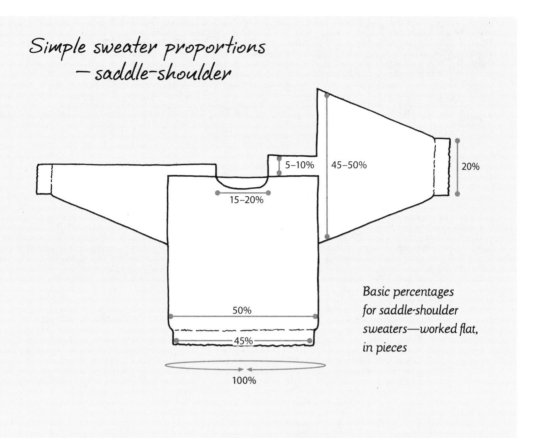

Simple sweater proportions — saddle-shoulder

5–10% 45–50% 20%

15–20%

50%

45%

100%

Basic percentages for saddle-shoulder sweaters—worked flat, in pieces

Sleeves, for all three styles

There is a range of percentages given for the sleeves. The smaller number will produce slimmer sleeves and the larger one will produce looser sleeves. Choose the percentage that is appropriate for the body style or fit preferences of the intended wearer.

Proportions: the easier way

My preliminary work for this book was based on ideas presented by Meg Swansen and Priscilla Gibson-Roberts (see bibliography on page 172). If you know about EPS (Elizabeth's Percentage System), you're aware that Elizabeth Zimmermann introduced this way of thinking about sweaters to many contemporary knitters.

The proportions I use are based on Priscilla Gibson-Roberts' *Knitting in the Old Way*. They are given here so you understand the basis for the working process explained in this book.

On my worksheets, you'll discover that I've simplified further, generally coming up with the appropriate sweater proportions by dividing the body circumference by 2, 3, 4, or 5 instead of working with percentages.

As you become familiar with this style of knitting, you can refine the proportions and methods to suit your own preferences.

Standard sizes

Children							
Size		**4**	**6**	**8**	**10**	**12**	**14**
Chest	inches	23	25	26 ½	28	30	31 ½
	cm	58.5	63.5	67.5	71	76	80
Back waist to neck	inches	9 ½	10 ½	12 ½	14	15	15 ½
	cm	24	26.5	32	35.5	38	39.5
Sleeve length to underarm	inches	10 ½	11 ½	12 ½	13 ½	15	16
	cm	26.5	29	32	34.5	38	40.5

Women							
Size		**XS**	**S**	**M**	**L**	**XL**	**XXL**
Bust	inches	28–30	32–34	36–38	40–42	44–46	48–50
	cm	71–76	81–86	91.5–96.5	101.5–106.5	112–117	122–127
Back waist to neck	inches	16 ½	17	17 ¼	17 ½	17 ¾	18
	cm	42	43	44	44.5	45	45.5
Sleeve length to underarm	inches	16 ½	17	17	17 ½	17 ½	18
	cm	42	43	43	44.5	44.5	45.5

Men						
Size		**S**	**M**	**L**	**XL**	**XXL**
Chest	inches	34–36	38–40	42–44	46–48	50–52
	cm	86–91.5	96.5–101.5	106.5–112	117–122	127–132
Back waist to neck	inches	25	26 ½	27	27 ½	28 ½
	cm	63.5	67.5	68.5	70	72.5
Sleeve length to underarm	inches	18	18 ½	19 ½	20	20 ½
	cm	45.5	47	49.5	51	52

Adapted, with minor modifications, from www.yarnstandards. com, compiled by Craft Yarn Council of America.

The sample sweaters

I've chosen simple numbers to display the calculations for the examples in this book. Most are based on a gauge of 5 stitches to 1 inch (20 stitches to 10 cm).

Most of the examples also show a 40-inch (102-cm) sweater, because at 5 stitches to the inch that size results in a nice, neat 200 stitches for the main number of stitches. This makes it easy to see what I am doing with the calculations. Because of differences in ease (see the table below), the same 40-inch sweater will relate as follows to people with the chest/bust measurements noted:

40-inch (102 cm): very close fit
38–39-inch (96–100 cm): close fit
36–38-inch (92–96 cm): standard fit
34–36-inch (86–92 cm): loose fit
34-inch (86 cm) or smaller: oversized

Of course, you'll be able to design sweaters to any size and silhouette you choose. That's the point of this approach to knitting!

Ease

Desired fit	Sweater measurement at chest/bust (adjust from body chest/bust measurement)	
Very close fit	Actual chest/bust measurement or less	*Note:* You'll see there's some overlap in the amounts of ease. For example, 2″ (5 cm) can result in either standard or close fit, or 4″ (10 cm) can result in either loose or standard fit. Smaller sizes need less ease than larger sizes to achieve the more generous fit designations. Thicker yarns generally need more ease as well because the yarn bulk itself takes up some of what would be ease room.
Close fit	+ 1–2″ (2.5–5 cm)	
Standard fit	+ 2–4″ (5–10 cm)	
Loose fit	+ 4–6″ (10–15 cm)	
Oversized	+ 6″ or more (15 cm or more)	

A few basics

If you haven't knitted sweaters with shaped yokes and shoulders before, this chapter will introduce you to a few techniques that you'll be using in the sweaters and other projects. Skim these over now, if you are so inclined, or reference these pages when you need the information.

Note: If you've never knitted in the round at all, the first book in this series, *Ethnic Knitting Discovery,* will give you a tour of the basic techniques you need to know for circular knitting.

Raglan, yoke, and saddle-shoulder sweaters are made with the same supplies as other knitting projects. Stitch markers make it easier to keep track of the shaping on the yoke, and spare needles, stitch holders, or scraps of yarn are used to place stitches on hold at various steps along the way.

You will find that certain kinds of yarns are better for specific projects. In each project, I provide yarn suggestions.

The following guidelines will give you a few additional tips for selecting yarn and needles.

Knitting needles, and some tricks for using them

When knitting in the round on a circular needle, the needle must be shorter than the circumference of your knitting so the stitches can reach around the needle without stretching. When a knitted piece becomes so small that it no longer fits on a 16-inch (40-cm) circular needle, I switch to double-pointed needles. I have so far found circular needles shorter than 16 inches (40 cm) uncomfortable to work with. The flexibility of the cable and the length of the points make an enormous difference on these shorter needles; because needle designs

This chapter explains a few basic knitting techniques. If you prefer, skip ahead to the projects and come back if you need specific help.

keep changing, you may find some short circular needles that work for you.

Recently a couple of new circular knitting techniques have become popular with knitters who don't like double-pointed needles. I learned them from people in my classes. With these techniques, you can knit a small tube on circular needles that are longer than the circumference of the fabric.

Knitting with two circular needles

Divide your stitches evenly onto two circular needles so the first needle holds the first half of the round and the second needle holds the second half of the round. To knit a round, using the first needle only, knit the first half of the round. Then turn the work around so the second half of the round is facing you, and switch to the second needle only to knit the second half of the round. Each set of stitches always stays on the same needle.

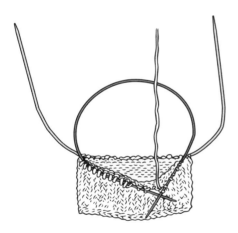

The dark blue needle is working the front set of stitches. The light blue needle and back set of stitches are in resting position.

Needle sizes

U.S.	Metric
0	2 mm
1	2.25 or 2.5 mm
2	2.75 or 3 mm
3	3.25 mm
4	3.5 mm
5	3.75 mm
6	4 mm
7	4.5 mm
8	5 mm
9	5.5 mm
10	6 mm
10½	6.5 mm
11	8 mm
13	9 mm
15	10 mm

Sources: www.yarnstandards. com, Craft Yarn Council of America, supplemented with manufacturers' specifications.

"Magic-loop" knitting

Put all of the stitches onto one long circular needle. Count across half of your stitches, and pull the cable of the circular needle out between the two groups of stitches.

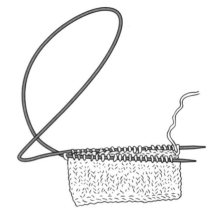

*Hold the needle tips parallel, pointing to the right, with the cable pulled out between the groups of stitches extending to the left. Push the stitches up onto the needle tips. The working yarn should be attached to the group of stitches on the back needle tip.

Pull the needle tip in the back out toward the right, sliding the stitches onto the cable. There will now be two cable loops, one on each side of the knitting. Use the needle tip that you just pulled free from the back to knit across the stitches on the front needle tip.

Turn the work around and repeat from *.

Yarn

Yarn comes in many different weights, or thicknesses. The weights have traditional names such as worsted, Aran, and DK, which can be confusing to the new knitter. A few years ago, several yarn companies and knitting publishers got together and standardized names for different yarn thicknesses. They developed a system of seven different yarn weights, ranging from thinner to thicker. Many yarn labels now show these standardized yarn weights to help make choosing yarns easier.

These categories include yarns in a range of gauges, so be careful to check the actual recommended gauge when choosing yarns. A yarn that knits up at 4½ stitches per inch (18 stitches per 10 cm) is quite a bit heavier than a yarn that knits up at 5 stitches per inch (20 stitches per 10 cm), yet both of these yarns are considered "medium weight" according to the new guidelines. Fortunately, when you design your own sweaters, you knit to your own gauge!

Children's sweaters are often made out of thinner yarns than adults' sweaters, to match the small body size. Adult sweaters may be made from very thin yarns for lightweight, sophisticated sweaters to very thick yarns for super-bulky sports sweaters. In general, the thicker the yarn you use, the more loosely the sweater should fit. Adding a couple of extra inches to the size of a bulky sweater allows the heavy fabric to flow freely and prevents the sweater from feeling like a straitjacket.

The yarn estimates in the chart on the next page are for sweaters knitted in one color in stockinette stitch or a lightly textured pattern. You will need 20 to 30 percent more yarn for a densely textured sweater, like an Aran with cables. When using multiple colors, you will need 20 to 30 percent more yarn, divided up between the

Yarn guidelines

Yarn weight	1	2	3	4	5	6
Type of yarn	Sock, fingering, or baby	Sport, baby	DK, light worsted	Worsted, Aran	Chunky	Bulky
Gauge range: stitches in 4 inches (10 cm) in stockinette stitch	27–32	23–26	21–24	16–20	12–15	6–11
Suggested U.S. needle size	1–3	3–5	5–7	7–9	9–11	11 or larger
Suggested metric needle side	2.25–3.25 mm	3.25–3.75 mm	3.75–4.5 mm	4.5–5.5 mm	5.5–8 mm	8 mm or larger

All specifications are suggested starting points for determining appropriate gauges and needle sizes. Your own gauge swatch will be your true guide. Information on this page adapted from www.yarnstandards.com, Craft Yarn Council of America. Size 0 is not listed here because it's usually not used by today's knitters for sweaters.

Approximate yarn quantities

Child's sweater	Chest 26–34″ (66–86 cm)	
Lightweight yarn	1000–1800 yards	900–1700 meters
Medium-weight yarn	900–1200 yards	850–1100 meters
Heavy-weight yarn	700–1000 yards	650-900 meters
Woman's hip-length sweater	Bust 32–44″ (81–112 cm)	
Lightweight yarn	1500–2600 yards	1400–2400 meters
Medium-weight yarn	1100–1700 yards	1000–1600 meters
Heavy-weight yarn	1000–1100 yards	900–1000 meters
Man's hip-length sweater	Chest 36–50″ (91–127 cm)	
Lightweight yarn	1800–3000 yards	1700–2750 meters
Medium-weight yarn	1500–2000 yards	1400–1850 meters
Heavy-weight yarn	1300–1500 yards	1200–1400 meters

These yarn estimates are for sweaters knitted in one color in stockinette stitch or a lightly textured pattern.

Adapted from Vicki Square, The Knitter's Companion, *and Ann Budd,* The Knitter's Handy Guide to Yarn Requirements.

colors. You will have to estimate based on how much of each color you plan to use in your design. When knitting an oversized, plus size, or extra-long sweater, you will need more yarn.

Always buy more yarn than you think you will need. Check with your yarn shop about its return policy. Most shops will allow you to return extra yarn for credit within one year of your purchase. You can always make a hat and scarf to match your sweater if you decide not to return the extra balls.

Increases and decreases

To shape your knitting, you add (increase) or remove (decrease) stitches to make the knitted piece get wider or narrower.

There are many different ways to increase and decrease. The following methods are my favorites. They work in a variety of situations and are quite easy to knit.

If you prefer a different method, feel free to substitute another technique in the projects.

Increases

Knit in front and back

The simplest way to increase is by knitting twice into the same stitch. This does leave a small bump on the right side of the work, so it is not a good choice when invisible increases are required.

1. Knit into the front of the next stitch. Do not drop the old stitch from the needle.

2. Knit into the back of the same stitch. Drop the old stitch from the needle. Two new stitches have been made.

Make 1 (M1)

This increase allows you to add a new stitch between two existing stitches. It is almost invisible, and works in almost any situation where you need to add a stitch.

1. With the tip of the left needle moving from front to back, lift the strand between the last stitch worked and the next stitch on the needle. Place the strand onto the left needle.

2. Knit into the back of the newly created loop to "make one" new stitch.

Note: If you don't knit into the back of the loop to twist the stitch, there will be a hole in your knitting.

Lifted increase

The lifted increase is another invisible increase. In this technique, you knit into the back of a stitch from the previous row to add a new stitch to the current row.

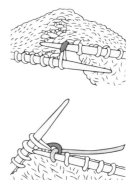

1. On the back (wrong side) of the work, insert the tip of the right needle into the top edge of the next stitch on the previous row.

2. Knit into this loop. You have added one stitch. Continue knitting across the row normally.

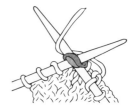

Decreases

Knit two together (k2tog)

This decrease slants to the right. To work it, knit two stitches together as though they were one stitch.

1. Insert the needle through two loops on the left needle at once, and work them together as a regular knit stitch.

Slip-slip-knit (SSK)

To make a mirror-image decrease that slants to the left, you must first turn the two stitches around on the needle, then knit them together.

1. Slip the next two stitches one at a time to the right needle as if to knit.

2. Insert the left needle into the fronts of the stitches and knit the two stitches together through the back loops with the right needle.

Sewing seams

Some sweaters are knitted with absolutely no sewing required, but others are made with flat pieces that must be sewn together. Even when you knit a sweater in the round, you may want to sew the shoulder seams together or join the underarm stitches with a seam. You can do both of these things by binding off stitches together, but that leaves a visible line. The following seams can be used to create invisible joins.

Invisible grafting

Invisible grafting is most often used to join two "live" sets of stitches, or open loops, together. It is also called kitchener stitch. Each of the two groups of stitches you plan to join must have the same number of stitches.

Break off the working yarn, leaving a strand long enough to work all the way across the join; this will generally be between three and four times the length of the join. Be generous in your estimate. Thread this working strand into a sewing-style yarn needle that has a blunt point.

1. (Setup) Hold the two pieces together on the two knitting needles, wrong sides facing, positioned so the working strand comes from the righthand stitch on the front needle. Insert the sewing needle into the first stitch on the back needle as if to knit, but don't take the stitch off its needle.

   Now insert the sewing needle into the first stitch on the front needle as if to purl, and again don't take the stitch off the needle.

2. (Back needle) Take the sewing needle to the back needle and insert it in the first stitch as if to purl—now remove that stitch from its needle.

   Insert the sewing needle into the next stitch as if to knit but do not remove it.

3. (Front needle) Take the sewing needle to the front needle and insert it in the first stitch as if to knit—now remove that stitch from its needle.

   Insert the sewing needle into the next stitch as if to purl but do not remove it.

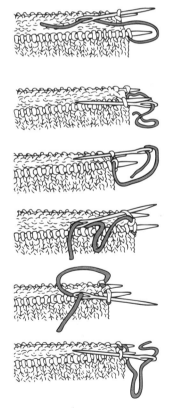

Repeat steps 2 and 3 until one stitch remains on each needle. Follow the established pattern as well as possible with these two stitches. One will be removed from its needle after the second pass of the sewing needle; there will be no second stitch on that needle to go through before moving to the other needle. The final stitch will only be entered once with the sewing needle. Fasten off.

Mattress stitch

Invisible seams, also known as mattress stitch seams, are sewn with the right side of the work facing up. This seam joins rows to rows and is used to sew side seams in sweaters that have been knitted flat.

1. With their right sides facing up, place the two pieces to be seamed on a flat surface.

2. With a tapestry needle and matching yarn, go under the bar between the first and second stitches near the edge of one piece of knitting. (Make your stitches a half-stitch in from the edge when working with bulky yarn and a full stitch in from the edge when working with medium- or light-weight yarn.)

3. Repeat step 2 on the other piece.

4. Continue to work from side to side, moving up one stitch each time and pulling gently on the yarn to close the seam after every few stitches.

After you gently tighten the stitches, they will disappear completely between the two pieces of knitting. Don't pull the seam too tight. The seam should be at a similar tension to that of the knitting.

For all of the seams, you will (of course) use matching yarn or thread. Our examples have been made with contrasting yarn so you can see the stitches.

End-to-end seam

This seam is used to join stitches to stitches when you need to sew cast-on or bound-off edges together, such as when sewing the shoulder seams on a sweater that has been knitted flat.

1. With the right sides of the fabric facing up, place the two pieces to be seamed on a flat surface.

2. With a tapestry needle and matching yarn, catch the knit V just inside the edge of one piece of knitting.

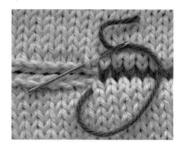

3. Repeat step 2 on the other piece.

4. Continue to work from side to side, pulling gently on the yarn to close the seam after you make each stitch.

The seam should be at the same tension as your knitting, and should look like a row of stockinette stitch.

End-to-side seam

When sewing sleeves into armholes, which require you to sew rows to stitches, you combine mattress stitch with end-to-end seaming.

Many books recommend a backstitch seam for sewing in sleeves. I don't like to backstitch my seams because you need to work from the wrong side and you can't see what you're doing, it's difficult to pick out the stitches if you don't like the results and want to start over, and it creates a bulky ridge around the armhole.

Short-row shaping

Sweaters knitted in the round with raglan or yoke shaping sometimes ride up in the back. I am not sure why this happens but it is easy to adjust by adding a few extra short rows to the back just before you join the arms and body together to knit the yoke. People with some body types love sweaters made with these short-row adjustments.

A short row is simply a row that has fewer stitches than the full piece of knitting. The same technique can be used at the top of the yoke to raise the back neck and create a neckline that fits more closely.

Different designers have different ideas about where to place short rows. This is my method; experiment to discover what works for you.

The instructions for projects 2 and 3 (raglan sweaters) and 5 and 6 (yoke sweaters) refer to optional short-row shaping to lengthen the body and contour the back shoulder and neck area. I suggest working short rows in plain-color sections of the body. It can be extremely challenging to coordinate patterning in combination with this technique.

Basic short-row technique

Turning in the middle of the row leaves a small hole. There are a number of ways to eliminate the holes at the turning points. One of those ways involves wrapping the turning stitch.

When instructions tell you to "wrap-and-turn":

1. Work to the turning point.

2. Wrap: Slip the next stitch onto the right needle as if to purl, bring the yarn to the front, and slip the same stitch back to the left needle. Take the yarn to the back of the work again.

3. Turn the work and knit or purl the next stitch.

This wrap-and-turn technique creates a float on the right side of the work. On the next complete row, you will work back over the wrapped stitch.

4. Knit the wrap together with the corresponding stitch on the lefthand needle to close up the holes created by the short-row shaping.

Short-row shaping for the body (lengthening the back)

Work 3 or 4 sets of short rows (6 or 8 rows) for worsted-weight yarn (more sets than this for very fine yarn, fewer for very bulky yarn).

To work a short-row set to lengthen the back of a pullover, begin at one side marker and follow this sequence:

Row 1 (right side): Knit to the last 3 stitches before the next side marker (the section you are now in will be the sweater back). Wrap and turn (see page 28).

Row 2 (wrong side): Purl to the last 3 stitches before the next side marker. Wrap and turn.

Repeat rows 1 and 2 another 2 or 3 times, each time working 2 or 3 fewer stitches before the wrap and turn.

Return to knitting in the round, remembering to hide the wrapped stitches when you come to them (see above).

Mark this side of the sweater as the back and continue with regular stockinette.

On a cardigan, the beginning-of-round marker will be at the center front. Work to the first side marker before starting the short-row shaping to ensure that you are working the short rows on the back of the sweater.

Short-row shaping at the back neck (accommodating the shoulders)

Work back-neck short rows when the yoke is 2 inches (5 cm) less than the yoke depth. To raise the back neck, work 3 or 4 sets of short rows for worsted-weight yarn (more sets than this for very fine yarn, fewer for very bulky yarn).

Begin at the contrasting marker, which is located at the beginning of the back yoke stitches. (On a cardigan, the beginning-of-round marker will be at the center front. Work to the marker at the beginning of the back yoke stitches and you'll be in the right location.)

Pullover

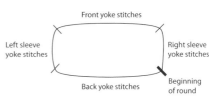

Front yoke stitches

Left sleeve yoke stitches

Right sleeve yoke stitches

Back yoke stitches

Beginning of round

Cardigan

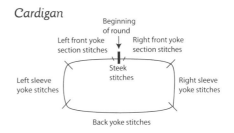

Beginning of round

Left front yoke section stitches

Right front yoke section stitches

Steek stitches

Left sleeve yoke stitches

Right sleeve yoke stitches

Back yoke stitches

Work across the back yoke stitches and the left sleeve stitches. You are at the marker that indicates the beginning of the front yoke stitches.

Row 1 (right side): Slip the marker for the front yoke stitches, knit a few more stitches (½–1 inch / 1.25–2.5 cm), and wrap and turn (see page 28).

Row 2 (wrong side): Purl to the right front marker (you'll have purled all the way across the left sleeve, back yoke, and right sleeve). Slip the marker, purl the same number that you knitted after the marker in row 1, and wrap and turn.

Repeat rows 1 and 2 another 2 or 3 times, each time working 2 or 3 fewer stitches before the wrap and turn. **AT THE SAME TIME,** continue to work raglan decreases on the appropriate rows. After the first couple of sets of short rows, you won't be slipping the marker any more because you'll be turning in the sleeve area, rather than the front.

When you have done as many short-row sets as you would like, return to knitting in the round, remembering to hide the wrapped stitches when you come to them.

Centering patterns

When working with color and texture patterns, you may want to center the designs on the body or sleeves of your sweater. It is your choice whether to center or not. Small patterns often look fine without centering, but large patterns will look better if they are centered.

When working with horizontal patterns, arrange the pattern so the design is centered on both the front and back of the sweater, making sure any partial repeats are located at the underarm "seams." Patterns on cardigans look best if they are centered around the front opening.

Adjusting stitch counts for horizontal patterns
The easiest way to center a pattern is to make sure your garment as a whole is worked on a stitch count that is a multiple of the pattern. Round your required number of stitches up or down to the nearest multiple. If you work with several patterns in one sweater, increase or decrease a few stitches in a plain row of knitting before

starting each new pattern so that the overall count is a multiple of the new pattern.

For example, if you are working with a chart that has a 12-stitch repeat, you need a total number of stitches that is a multiple of 12 such as 216, 240, or 264.

If you are working with 216 stitches and your next pattern has a multiple of 10 stitches, you need to have 220 stitches for the new pattern. So you increase 4 stitches on a plain row before starting the new pattern. If you had 264 stitches, you would need to decrease 4 stitches to 260. If you had 240 stitches, you would not have to increase or decrease because 240 is evenly divisible by both 12 and 10.

If you are working on a sleeve, where the stitch count changes frequently, don't worry about having the right number of stitches. Just center the patterns on the starting count and work the edges of the patterns into the changing counts as best you can. It's easiest to do this on a sleeve that is worked from the shoulder down to the cuff, because the pattern is established and the decreases simply nibble away at the outer repeats as the sleeve narrows. But you can also do it on a sleeve that is worked from the cuff up to the shoulder by slowly adding pattern sections on each side of the increases.

Centering patterns on cardigans

It is easiest to round the number of stitches in the pieces of your cardigan up or down to an even multiple of your pattern, but sometimes this may cause the sweater to be too large or too small for your taste.

If you are not working with an even multiple of your pattern in each piece of the garment, center the pattern around the front opening of the sweater for a professional look. (See pages 166–168.)

Some patterns have isolated motifs that are scattered on a solid background. To center these patterns when your main number of stitches is not an even multiple of the pattern repeat, first determine how many extra stitches you will have. In the example shown, the repeat is 12 stitches. If you have 128 stitches, you will have 10 full repeats plus 8 stitches left over ($12 \times 10 = 120 + 8 = 128$).

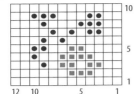 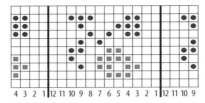

Centering a series of motifs

Half of the extra stitches (4) will go on each end of the round or row. Beginning at the center front, which will be the beginning of the row if you are working back and forth or just after the steek stitches if you are working in the round, work the last 4 stitches of the repeat, then work the full repeats of 12 stitches until you reach the last 4 stitches, then work the first 4 stitches of the chart once more, just before the center front opening or steek stitches. In the second chart, the first and last 4 stitches are drawn in, to illustrate how this pattern is centered by using partial repeats.

Some patterns have the repeat arranged so that the pattern flows seamlessly around a piece of circular knitting. To center these patterns, you simply repeat a stitch or a few stitches at one edge of the repeat on the other end, as shown in the sample chart. In this case, you need a multiple of 6, plus 3 to balance. Because this is a fairly small chart, you should be able to easily round your main number of stitches up or down to fit the pattern.

Set up the pattern as follows: Beginning at the center front, which will be the beginning of the row if you are working back and forth or just after the steek stitches if you are working in the round, work the pattern repeat of 6 stitches all the way around to the last 3 stitches, then repeat the first 3 stitches of the pattern one last time. These 3 stitches are added in the chart on the right below.

Centering a pattern intended to flow seamlessly in the round

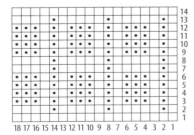 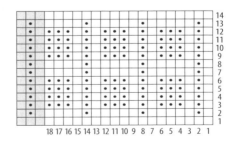

Abbreviations and symbols

Knitting patterns are often full of abbreviations intended to save space. I have used some abbreviations in the instructions in this book, but have tried to keep them to a minimum.

Although abbreviations are not completely standardized, the table shows some common ones.

Symbols are even less standardized than abbreviations. Always check the key before knitting.

Symbols used in color charts

Symbol	
☐	MC = main (background) color
⬤	CC1 = pattern color 1
▣	CC2 = pattern color 2

Symbols used in knit-and-purl charts

Symbol	Worked in the round	Worked back and forth
☐	knit	knit on right side purl on wrong side
⊡	purl	purl on right side knit on wrong side

See also detailed cable symbols on page 120.

Abbreviations

Term	Definition
cm	centimeter
cn or Cn	cable needle
dec	decrease
dpn(s)	double-pointed needle(s)
inc	increase
k or K	knit
k2tog	knit two together
M1	make one
p or P	purl
pm	place marker
rnd	round
RS	right side
sl	slip
SSK	slip one, slip one, knit the two slipped stitches together through their back loops
st(s)	stitch(es)
St st	stockinette stitch
wyib	with yarn in back
wyif	with yarn in front
WS	wrong side

Lithuania

I am half Lithuanian, so when I saw a book on Lithuanian knitting on the Internet I wanted to buy it right away. The only problem was that I could only find one place that was selling the book and no one at that site spoke any English. I kept searching on the web and finally found a copy on eBay. There was no "buy now" button, so I placed my bid and crossed my fingers, hoping that no one would outbid me at the last minute.

I was lucky. Two weeks later, *Lietuvininkų Pirštinės (Gloves of Lithuania Minor)* was delivered to my front door.

Although I knew of several books about knitting from the Baltic countries of Latvia and Estonia, I had never seen a book about Lithuanian knitting before. The book I discovered is filled with charts and photos of gloves and mittens that were made in the nineteenth and twentieth centuries, as well as a treasury of stories about the history of knitting in the Baltic region.

Sweaters are made in Lithuania today, but they were not part of the traditional clothing worn by women or men. Gloves, however, have been very important in traditional Lithuanian culture for centuries. In the cold climate of Lithuania, mittens do a much better job than gloves at keeping hands and fingers warm, but gloves were used to celebrate the major passages in life. Made with striped ribbing and with color patterns on the cuffs, hands, and fingers, festively decorated gloves were given as gifts and blessings to family members and loved ones.

In the past, many Lithuanians believed that gloves had magical or supernatural power. In the nineteenth century, gloves were put onto the hands of the dead, perhaps to make the recipients more comfortable in the afterlife. Women knitted gloves in anticipation of their own funerals, as well as for the imminent funerals of loved ones. Gloves were also commonly given to grave diggers and coffin carriers at funerals. During a funeral, a woman from the family would slip a pair of gloves into the coffin carriers' and grave diggers' jackets, so the garments could be seen by all who attended the burial.

Most gloves, however were given away at more festive occasions. At weddings, gloves were provided as gifts to all of the wedding guests, or sometimes just to the bridegroom's parents, relatives, and servants. Often a bride would also give gloves to the bridegroom when the couple exchanged rings, and would leave a pair at the altar during the wedding ceremony. The bride would also place pairs of gloves on her father-in-law's and the matchmaker's shoulders during the wedding. The men in the bridal party would wear the gloves received by the bride on their shoulders, so all of the guests could see the colorful gifts. Young girls placed a pair of gloves on their dancing partners' shoulders. The members of the bridal party would give gloves to the bride and groom, and often attached them to a wreath.

After the wedding, the bride would leave gloves in the cattle shed and the barn to ensure that her house would be in order and to show that she would be a good housewife. When she visited her mother-in-law for the first time, she would leave gloves and a woven sash in

In traditional Lithuanian culture, gloves were used to celebrate the major passages in life.

CHAPTER 3 HIGHLIGHTS

Skills
☑ *Working with two or three colors*

Techniques
☑ *Striped ribbing*
☑ *Modifying color patterns*

Garment styling
☑ *All pieces worked in the round*
☑ *Raglan construction*

the bath to show her wish to bring grandchildren into the family. At christenings, gloves were often given to the baby's godparents and the priest; the priest received more gloves at the child's confirmation.

Today, these traditions and many others have become faded memories, living on only in the recollections of a few older knitters and in the stitches of the few remaining gloves that have been preserved in museums and hope chests.

The pattern stitches I've included in this chapter come from gloves knitted in Lithuania during the twentieth century. As a way of carrying on the tradition in a different form, I have adapted them for use on raglan sweaters.

Techniques

Striped ribbing

Lithuanian mittens and gloves are often made with bright, multicolored ribbing. This fancy ribbing also works well on sweaters, adding a fun and festive look. Work no more than 2 to 4 rounds in each color, so you can run the unused colors up the inside of the ribbing at the beginnings of the rounds. To tie down vertical floats, catch any unused strands of yarn with the working strand at the beginning of each row.

After you finish working the ribbing, you will have only two ends for each color: one for its start and one for its conclusion. Weave in the ends vertically on the wrong side. If you weave in the ends horizontally, you might stretch and distort the ribbing and reduce its elasticity. Don't worry that you are not working each end solely into stitches knitted with the same color.

Seen from the front, the unused colors disappear in the edge rib. This is knit 2, purl 1 ribbing.

From the back, you can see the colors stranded up the beginnings of the rows.

Working with two or three colors

There are many different ways to carry your yarn as you knit.

When working with multiple colors—especially when you are managing more than two colors in the same row—if you knit Continental-style, you can carry all of the colors over the fingers of your left hand. This way, you can "pick" the color that you need for each stitch, without constantly dropping and picking up different strands of yarn.

If you knit English-style (carrying the yarn or yarns in your right hand), you can drop and pick up the colors as needed, although this will make your knitting go more slowly.

If you already know another way to knit with multiple colors, feel free to use that technique.

To change from color A to color B, drop the working yarn (A) and bring the new color (B, new working yarn) on top of A. Knit as many stitches as you need.

To change back to A from color B, drop B and bring A under B. Begin using A again. Knit as many stitches as you need.

* If you plan to carry the unused yarn for more than about an inch, control the floats by weaving in the stranded yarn. I describe one way of doing this in Ethnic Knitting Discovery *on pages 104–105.*

Pattern stitches

These Lithuanian pattern stitches are from *Gloves of Lithuania Minor* by Irena Regina Merkienė and Marija Pautieniūtė-Banionienė. I have chosen patterns that convey the personality of the region and that adapt well to use on sweaters.

Birds and Hearts Border

This pattern has a large horizontal repeat of 48 stitches. It's so charming it's worth the effort of experimenting with yarn choice (gauge) and sizing to get it to work out for you. You can separate the birds and hearts by another column of stitches to expand it slightly if you need to.

Repeat: 48 stitches by 17 rows

Lithuania Minor (Mažoji Lietuva)

The cultural area known as Lithuania is made up of five ethnographic regions: Aukštaitija, Dzūkija, Suvalkija, Žemaitija, and Mažoji Lietuva.

The patterns that I offer in this section come from Mažoji Lietuva, also called Lithuania Minor.

The political history of this part of the world has been complex. Located along the Baltic Sea, Lithuania Minor was part of Prussia until 1945. Today some sections of this ethnographic unit are under the political umbrella of the country of Lithuania and some are included in Poland and Russia.

Star Border

This chart includes edge stitches to help you center the pattern. Work the first 13 stitches, work the repeat as many times as needed, and end with the last 4 stitches. If the repeat fits perfectly into your stitch count, ignore the edge stitches.

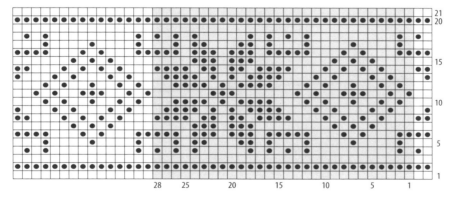

Repeat: 28 stitches plus edge stitches (2 at beginning, 15 at end) by 21 rows

Lily Motif

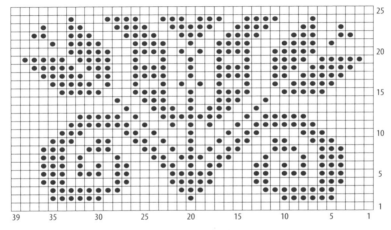

Repeat:
39 stitches
by 25 rows

For both the lily and the elk, see page 73 for information on working with large motifs.

Elk Motif

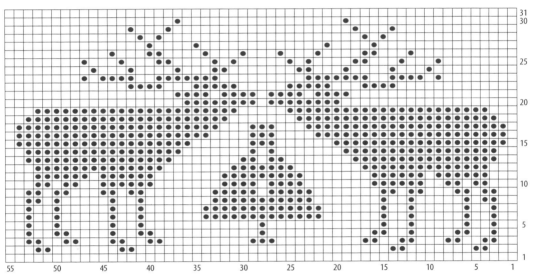

Repeat: 55 stitches by 31 rows

Flowers (all·over pattern)

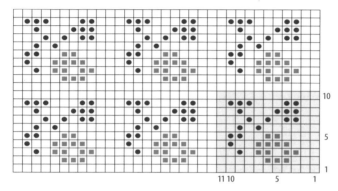

You can work the two patterns on this page right side up or upside down.

Repeat:
11 stitches
by 10 rows

Climbing Vines (all·over pattern)

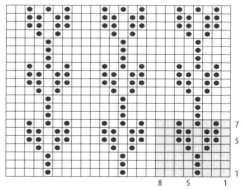

Repeat: 8 stitches by 7 rows

The names on these patterns are not traditional.

Blossom Border

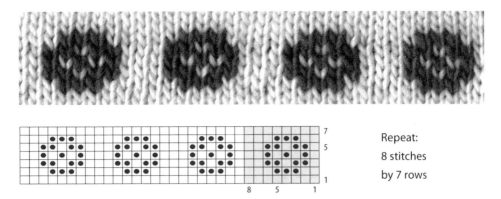

Repeat:
8 stitches
by 7 rows

Simple Border

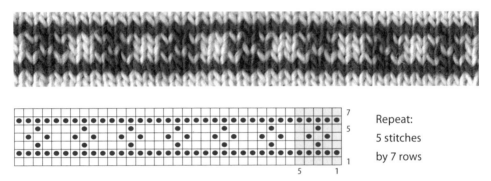

Repeat:
5 stitches
by 7 rows

Entertaining Geometric Border

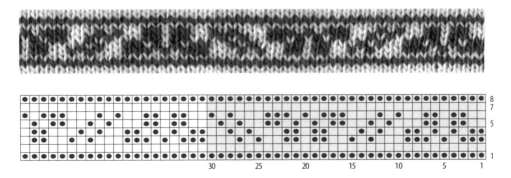

Repeat: 30 stitches by 8 rows

43

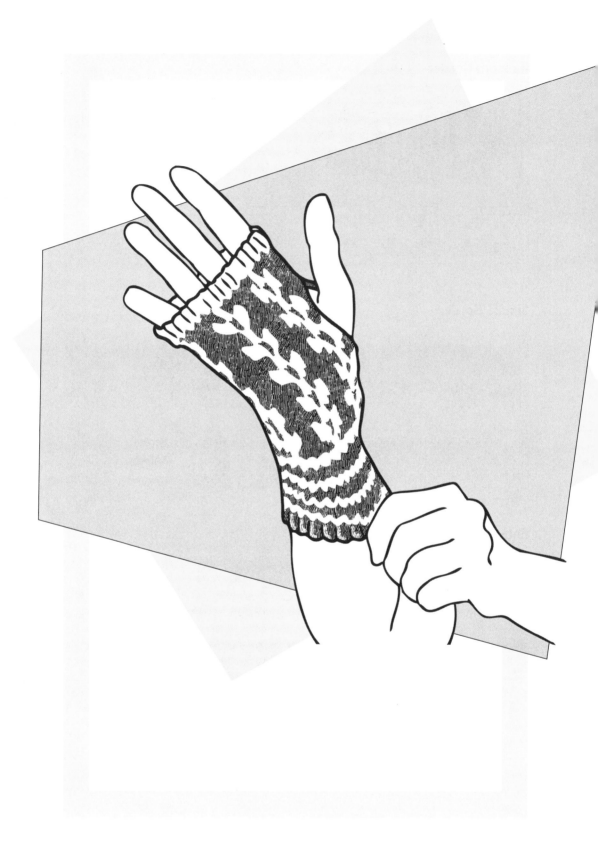

Fingerless Gloves

Traditional color patterns from Lithuania were most frequently used on gloves, mittens, and socks. These fingerless gloves are an easy version of a traditional design that lets you practice the color patterns. If you use the same yarn and needles as you plan to use in your sweater, the gloves can be used as your gauge swatch. Knit 2, purl 1 ribbing is very popular on gloves in Lithuania. You may want to experiment with that here.

✓ Striped ribbing
✓ Color patterns worked both in the round
   and back and forth

The example shows gloves in a women's medium, worked in a worsted-weight yarn at 5½ stitches to the inch (22 stitches to 10 cm).

Pattern: Climbing Vines (page 42).

The Flowers pattern (same page) will make absolutely charming fingerless gloves, if you'd like a small challenge in this project.

In order to have balanced patterns (three vertical repeats each on front and back), it will need to be worked at a gauge of about 9 stitches to the inch (36 stitches to 10 cm). You will also probably want a few additional plain stitches on either side of the thumb, so the patterned area has room to breathe around the thumb opening.

Get ready   *yarn & needles*

Yarn

Smooth yarn will show off these color patterns best. Wool is best for gloves, because the springy yarn knits up into an elastic fabric that will hold its shape and cling to your wrists.

Any weight of yarn will work, but for practice I suggest a medium-weight yarn and U.S. size 7 or 8 (4.5 or 5 mm) knitting needles. To fit a large motif on the back of the hand, you will need to use fine-weight yarn and U.S. size 0 or 1 (between 2 and 2.5 mm) knitting needles, or whatever gives you a gauge of about 8 stitches per inch (32 stitches to 10 cm).

You will need a total of approximately 400 yards (365 m) of medium-weight yarn or 500 yards (458 m) of fine-weight yarn for a pair of adult gloves.

Knitting needles

In a size appropriate for the yarn you've chosen:

✦ Double-pointed needles: set of 4 or 5

Two sizes smaller than primary needles:

✦ Double-pointed needles: set of 4 or 5 for ribbing

Needle guidelines, including tips on choosing lengths of circular needles and on working small tubes on circulars, if you would like to use them instead of double-points, are on pages 18–20.

Additional supply
✦ Stitch marker (optional)

Get set   *stitches, gauge & size*

Stitches and gauge

1 Select the pattern stitches for your gloves. Use the combination shown on the sample illustration (page 45), or choose your own combination of stitches either from this book or from a knitting stitch library.

2 Make a gauge swatch in each of the pattern stitches you have chosen.

It is a good idea to practice each pattern stitch to make sure you enjoy knitting it and to learn the pattern. That way you'll make any mistakes on your practice swatch instead of on your gloves.

3 Measure your gauge and record it on the planning worksheet on page 48.

Size

1 Choose a size for your gloves and write the measurements on the visual plan below and in the boxes on the planning worksheet on page 48.

★ Child: circumference 6½ inches (16.5 cm)

★ Women's medium: circumference 7½ inches (19 cm)

★ Women's large or men's medium: circumference 8½ inches (21.5 cm)

2 Use the calculations on the worksheet on page 48 to figure the remaining numbers before you start, or just calculate each new number as you need it.

3 Transfer the resulting numbers to the visual plan below or the step-by-step

instructions on page 49, depending on how much guiding detail you would like to have while you knit. The visual plan can be helpful even if you are using the step-by-step project sheet as a confidence builder.

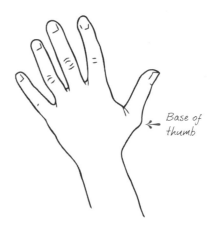

Base of thumb

Knit! *option I: using a visual plan*

Lithuania
Fingerless Gloves

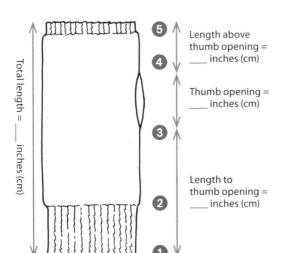

Total length = ____ inches (cm)

5 **4** Length above thumb opening = ____ inches (cm)

Thumb opening = ____ inches (cm)

3

Length to thumb opening = ____ inches (cm)

2

1

Circumference = ____ inches (cm)
Main number of stitches =
____ (gauge x circumference)

1 Cast on and work initial border

2 Set up pattern(s)

3 Form thumb opening

4 Work final border

5 Bind off

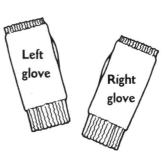

Left glove

Right glove

Knit! *option 2: using a planning worksheet*   Lithuania Fingerless Gloves

Measurements and stitch counts for project I

	Calculation	Example	Description
Stitch gauge	___ stitches = 1 inch or 1 cm	**5½ stitches =** 1 inch	**Stitch gauge** is critical for a good fit on fingerless gloves.
Circumference	___ inches (cm)	**7½ inches**	Desired **circumference** of a glove.
a *Main number of stitches*	___ x ___ = ___ stitches	5.5 x 7.5 = **41.25 stitches**	Multiply the stitch gauge by the circumference to calculate the **main number of stitches**.
		40 stitches	Round up or down to a multiple of your pattern stitch repeat. If you are using different patterns on the back of the hand and the palm, adjust the stitch count as necessary.
A *Length to thumb opening*	___ inches (cm)	**5 inches**	Desired **length** from cast-on edge **to thumb opening**. This is the distance from the base of your thumb to the wrist of the fingerless glove. How far past your wrist bone would you like the glove to extend?
B *Length of thumb opening*	___ inches (cm)	**2 inches**	Desired **length of thumb opening**. Measure the hand from the base of the thumb, just above the wrist, to the point where the thumb separates from the hand. It will usually be between 1½ and 2 inches (3.75 and 5 cm).
Length above thumb opening	___ inches (cm)	**2 inches**	Desired **length** from the top of the **thumb opening** to the bind-off edge. How far down your fingers would you like the glove to extend? This length generally falls anywhere between the knuckles at the bases of the fingers and the first knuckle on the little finger.
C *Total length*	___ + ___ + ___ = ___ inches	5 + 2 + 2 = **9 inches**	To get the **total length** of the glove, add length to thumb opening PLUS length of thumb opening PLUS length above opening.

Need a slightly different stitch count? Increase or decrease by a few.

Knit! *option 3: a step-by-step project sheet*

Lithuania
Fingerless Gloves

Do the calculations on the planning worksheet on page 48 so you have the numbers to fill in here.

 Cast on and work initial border

 With contrasting color and smaller needles, cast on **main number of stitches:** ____ stitches.

Distribute stitches evenly on 3 or 4 double-pointed needles. Being careful not to twist, join to knit in the round. Place a marker or use the yarn tail from the cast-on to keep track of the beginning of the round.

Work in striped ribbing, changing colors as desired, until ribbing measures 2 to 3 inches (5 to 7.5 cm), or desired length.

 Set up pattern(s)

Change to background color and larger needles. Follow chart to work the pattern stitch of your choice until gloves measure ____ inches (cm) (**length to thumb opening**).

 Form thumb opening

To form thumb opening, work to the end of the round and turn. Work back and forth, continuing to follow your pattern chart, until the thumb opening measures ____ inches (cm) (**length of thumb opening**).

Rejoin to work in the round. Work even until glove measures ½ inch (1.25 cm) less than ____ inches (cm) (**total length**).

 Work final border

Cut background color. With contrasting color and smaller needles, work ½ inch (1.25 cm) of ribbing.

5 **Bind off**

Bind off loosely. Weave in the ends.

Raglan Pullover with Border Pattern

This raglan sweater is made in three stages. First the body, decorated with a border pattern, is knitted in the round from the hem to the armholes, then set aside while the sleeves are worked to the underarms. Second, the sleeves are worked: decorated above the cuffs with the same border that appears on the body, they are then knitted plain to the armholes. Third, the pieces are joined together and the yoke is knitted. The border is worked again at the base of the yoke.

For a sporty look, you can knit the remainder of the yoke in the contrasting color. The multicolored striped ribbing and the simple Lithuanian-inspired border make this an easy, eye-catching garment.

- ✓ *Striped ribbing*
- ✓ *Balancing one pattern on sweater parts, and optional color blocking*
- ✓ *Lower body and sleeves worked in the round to the underarm, then joined so the yoke can be worked in the round*

The illustration shows a sweater with a 40-inch (102-cm) body circumference and 24-inch (61-cm) body length (including 2 inches [5 cm] of ribbing) in medium-weight yarn with 4¾ stitches and 7 rows to the inch (19 stitches and 28 rows to 10 cm). The 48-stitch birds-and-hearts band that I chose does not readily accommodate sizing adjustments, but I think it's wonderful. I got it to work for a 40-inch (102-cm) girth by using this gauge, but the repeat is going to be challenging for most sizes. If it doesn't work for your yarn and sizing, choose an alternative pattern that has a narrower repeat, like the ones on pages 39, 42, and 43.

Patterns: Birds and Hearts (page 38) and simple stripes.

Get ready *yarn & needles*

Yarn

This sweater can be made with any type of yarn. Wool or a wool blend will make a warm winter garment, while a sweater made of cotton can be worn in other seasons as well. As long as the yarn is smooth and comes in the colors you want, it will work well in this design.

Any weight of yarn will work, but for practice I suggest a medium-weight yarn and U.S. size 7 or 8 (4.5 or 5 mm) knitting needles.

Yarn guidelines, including a yardage estimate table, are on pages 20–22.

Knitting needles

In a size appropriate for the yarn you've chosen:

✦ Circular needle for body: for an adult sweater, use a needle at least 29 inches (74 cm) long

✦ Circular needle for sleeves and neckband: 16 inches (40 cm) long

✦ Double-pointed needles for cuffs: set of 4 or 5

Tip: Some knitters find that their gauge is more consistent if they knit the colorwork portions of a project on a needle that is one size larger than the needle they use for the solid areas. You may also prefer to use smaller needles (often two sizes smaller) when you work the ribbing on the body and the sleeve cuffs.

Needle guidelines, including tips on choosing lengths of circular needles and on working small tubes on circulars, are on pages 18–20.

Additional supplies
✦ Stitch markers
✦ Spare needle or stitch holders

Get set *stitches, gauge & size*

Stitches and gauge

1 Select the pattern stitches for your sweater. Use the combination shown in the illustration on page 51 or choose your own combination of stitches, from this book or from a knitting-stitch library.

2 Make a gauge swatch in stockinette stitch. Knit the swatch in the round to make sure you get an accurate gauge measurement. If you don't have a lot of experience with colorwork, make both a solid swatch and a colorwork swatch to see if you get the same gauge with the same size needle.

3 Measure your gauge. Write the stitch gauge and row gauge on the sweater-planning worksheet on page 55.

Size

1 Measure your favorite sweater or use the size charts on page 16 to determine the basic dimensions for your sweater. Write the measurements on the visual plan on page 54 and the sweater-planning worksheet on page 55.

2 Use the calculations on the worksheets on pages 55–57 to figure all the remaining numbers before you start, or just calculate each new number as you need it.

3 Transfer the resulting numbers to the visual plan on page 54 or the step-by-step instructions on pages 58–60, depending on how much guiding detail you would like to have while you knit.

Cover sweater story: Lithuanian-style pullover for a child   *by Debbie O'Neill*

I knew I wanted to make a girl's sweater for my daughter, and the Lithuanian floral motifs really caught my eye. I started out doing a lot of swatching to experiment with combinations of motifs and colors. I thought about doing the vine motif at the bottom of the sweater and the flowers on the yoke. I thought about doing several repeats of flowers and changing the shade with each repeat. In the end, I realized that my ideas were going to appear too busy on a little body.

I settled on a raglan-style pullover. Before casting on, I figured out how many stitches I needed to get the right size of sweater at my gauge. I then adjusted this stitch count

to accommodate the floral motif. I did the same math for the sleeves at the cuff. I did not work sleeve shaping in the portion of the sweater with colorwork, since it only consists of a few inches.

To add a bit more color, I worked stripes into all of the ribbings. I considered adding the floral motif to the yoke, but decided not to because I was worried about overwhelming this small sweater. It would also have been tricky to maintain the integrity of the motif while I was working raglan shaping.

I am pleased with all of my decisions: this simple sweater was fun to knit.

Knit! *option I: using a visual plan*

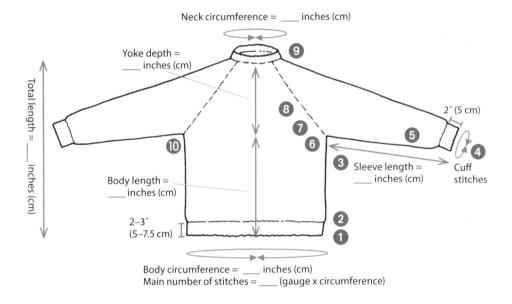

Neck circumference = ____ inches (cm)

Yoke depth = ____ inches (cm)

Total length = ____ inches (cm)

2″ (5 cm)

Sleeve length = ____ inches (cm)

Cuff stitches

Body length = ____ inches (cm)

2–3″ (5–7.5 cm)

Body circumference = ____ inches (cm)
Main number of stitches = ____ (gauge x circumference)

LOWER BODY

1. Cast on ____ stitches (stitches to cast on, or 90% of main number of stitches) and knit ribbing

2. Increase to ____ stitches (main number of stitches), change to stockinette stitch, and work border pattern

3. Work to body length and knit optional short rows

SLEEVES

4. Cast on ____ cuff stitches and knit ribbing

5. Work border at lower edge of sleeve; increase at even intervals along underarm to ____ sleeve stitches, then work even until sleeve reaches sleeve length

UPPER BODY

6. Join sleeves and body

7. Work border pattern on yoke

8. Begin raglan decreases every other round, and decrease to ____ neck stitches

FINISH

9. Work neckband and bind off

10. Join underarms and weave in ends

Knit! *option 2: using planning worksheets*
Lithuania
Sweater *with* Border Pattern

Measurements for project 2

	Calculation	Example	Description
Stitch gauge	____ stitches = 1 inch or 1 cm	**5** stitches = 1 inch	**Stitch gauge** is critical for knitting a sweater that fits properly.
Row gauge	____ rows = 1 inch or 1 cm	**6** rows = 1 inch	**Row gauge** is often important for raglan sweaters, because it can be used to calculate the placement of decreases. However, I prefer to fudge as I go!
Body width	____ inches (cm)	**20** inches	Measure the **width** of the sweater body.
Body circumference	____ x 2 = ____ inches (cm)	20 x 2 = **40** inches	Double the body width for the **circumference of the sweater**.
Total length	____ inches (cm)	**24** inches	Measure the **length** of the sweater body from cast-on to shoulder.
Sleeve length	____ inches (cm)	**18** inches	Measure the **sleeve length** from the cuff edge to the underarm.
Yoke depth	____ ÷ 2 = ____ inches (cm)	20 ÷ 2 = **10** inches	Divide the body width by 2 to calculate the **yoke depth**. (See tips on page 14 for altering yoke depth.)
Body length	____ – ____ = ____ inches (cm)	24 – 10 = **14** inches	Subtract the yoke depth from the total body length to calculate the **length of the body from the cast-on edge to the armhole**.
Upper sleeve circumference	____ x .40 = ____ inches (cm)	40 x .40 = **16** inches	Take 35 to 40 percent of the body circumference to calculate the **upper sleeve circumference**, depending on whether you want tighter (.35) or looser (.40) sleeves.
Neck circumference	____ inches (cm)	**14** inches	Measure the **circumference around the neck** or use the sweater proportions chart on page 14 to calculate the neck circumference.

Stitch counts for project 2

		Calculation	Example	Description
a	Main number of stitches	___ x ___ = ___ stitches	40 x 5 = **200** stitches	Multiply the body circumference by your stitch gauge to calculate the **main number of stitches**. Round this up or down as necessary to equal an even multiple of the pattern stitch you've chosen.
b	Stitches to cast on	___ x .9 = ___ stitches	200 x .9 = **180** stitches 180 stitches is a multiple of 4	Take 90 percent of the main number of stitches to calculate the **number of stitches to cast on**. Round up or down to a multiple of 4 stitches for working k2, p2 ribbing.
c	Front stitches & Back stitches	___ ÷ 2 = ___ stitches	200 ÷ 2 = **100** stitches	Divide the main number of stitches in half to determine the **number of stitches in the upper front and upper back.**
d	Sleeve stitches	___ x ___ = ___ stitches	16 x 5 = **80** stitches	Multiply the upper sleeve circumference by your stitch gauge to calculate the **number of sleeve stitches** required at the top of each sleeve.
e	Underarm stitches	___ x 2 = ___ stitches	5 x 2 = **10** stitches	Multiply your stitch gauge by 2 to calculate how many stitches to set aside for a 2-inch (5-cm) **underarm seam.** (Metric: Divide the number of stitches in 10 cm by 2 to reach the same number.)
f	Front yoke stitches & Back yoke stitches	___ – ___ = ___ stitches	100 – 10 = **90** stitches	Subtract the number of underarm stitches from the front/back stitches to calculate how many **stitches from the front and back** will remain for the **yoke.**
g	Sleeve yoke stitches	___ – ___ = ___ stitches	80 – 10 = **70** stitches	Subtract the number of underarm stitches from the sleeve stitches to calculate how many **stitches from each sleeve** will remain for the **yoke.**

This example has been set up with numbers that happen to result in an adult's sweater with a finished chest measurement of 40″ (102 cm) that falls to just below the waistline. If you're not that size, and only a few of us will be, use the guidelines on pages 14–17 and measurements you gather for yourself to make a sweater that is customized for its wearer.

Stitch counts for project 2 (continued)

	Calculation	Example	Description
h Total yoke stitches	___ + ___ + ___ + ___ = ___ stitches	90 + 90 + 70 + 70 = **320** stitches	To determine the **total number of stitches at the beginning of the yoke**, add front yoke stitches, back yoke stitches, left sleeve yoke stitches, and right sleeve yoke stitches.
i Neck stitches	___ x ___ = ___ stitches	14 x 5 = **70** **68** stitches is a multiple of 4	Multiply the neck circumference by the stitch gauge to calculate the **neck stitches**, which represent the number of stitches that remain after the yoke decreasing. Round this up or down to a multiple of 4 for working k2, p2 ribbing.
j Cuff stitches	___ stitches	**40** stitches 40 stitches is a multiple of 4	After you knit the body of your sweater, wrap the ribbing around your wrist and count the **number of stitches for the cuff**. For a rough estimate of this number, divide the main number of stitches by 5. Round up or down to a multiple of 4 for working k2, p2 ribbing

Need a slightly different stitch count? Increase or decrease by a few.

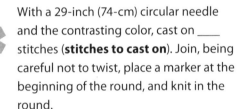

Knit! *option 3: a step-by-step project sheet*   Lithuania
Sweater *with* Border Pattern

Use this project sheet if you are not yet comfortable working directly from the sweater-planning diagram. With time, you'll find that you no longer need to refer to these instructions.

Do the calculations on the planning worksheets on pages 55–57 so you have the numbers to fill in here.

1 Cast on and knit ribbing

With a 29-inch (74-cm) circular needle and the contrasting color, cast on ____ stitches (**stitches to cast on**). Join, being careful not to twist, place a marker at the beginning of the round, and knit in the round.

Work in k2, p2 ribbing, adding main color and changing colors for stripes as desired (see striped ribbing on page 36), until the ribbing measures 2 or 3 inches (5 or 7.5 cm), or desired length.

2 Work border pattern

Use the main color and stockinette stitch (knit every round). Increase to ____ stitches (**main number of stitches**) on the first round as follows: *K9, increase 1, repeat from * to end of round. (Fudge if you need a few extra stitches to achieve a multiple of your border pattern.)

On the next round, knit ____ **back stitches**, place a second marker, knit to the end of the round (____ **front**

stitches). You now have a marker at the beginning of the round and a second marker halfway around, marking the side "seams" of the sweater.

Work even in stockinette stitch with the border and body patterns. Cut the contrasting color when you have completed the sequence of patterns, leaving ends long enough to weave in later.

3 Work lower body and optional short rows

With the main color, work even in stockinette until the body measures ____ inches (cm) (**body length**) from the cast-on edge.

Optional: See "short-row shaping for the body" on page 29.

On the next round, bind off or place on hold ____ **underarm stitches** at each side marker, with half of the underarm stitches coming before the marker and half after it. Remove the markers.

Set the body aside, placing its stitches on a spare needle or stitch holders.

4 Cast on and knit cuffs

Using double-pointed needles and contrasting color, cast on ____ stitches (**cuff stitches**). Join, being careful not to twist, place a marker at the beginning of the round, and knit in the round.

Work in k2, p2 ribbing, adding main color and changing colors for stripes as desired, until the ribbing measures 2 inches (5 cm), or desired length.

5 Work sleeve increases

Add main color and change to stockinette stitch. Work the border pattern, then cut the contrasting color and continue in stockinette stitch with the main color.

AT THE SAME TIME, begin increasing for the sleeve as follows: On every 4th round, k1, increase 1, knit to just before last stitch, increase 1, k1.

When the stitches no longer fit comfortably on the double-pointed needles, change to the 16-inch (40-cm) circular needle.

Keep an eye on the shape of your sleeve and measure it against your model sweater or try your sleeve on after every few inches (cm) to make sure the sleeve is increasing at a comfortable rate. If your sleeve is becoming wide too quickly, start increasing every 6th round. If it is not widening quickly enough, start increasing every 3rd round.

Continue increasing until you have ____ **sleeve stitches** and then work even until sleeve is ____ inches (cm) (**sleeve length**) from the cast-on edge.

On the next round, bind off or place on hold ____ **underarm stitches** at the marker, with half of the underarm stitches coming before the marker and half after it. Remove the marker.

Set the sleeve aside, placing its stitches on a spare needle or stitch holders.

Make second sleeve the same way as the first, steps 4 and 5.

6 Join sleeves and body

Arrange the body and sleeve stitches on one long circular needle, as follows: Slip ____ **back yoke stitches** onto the needle, place a marker. Slip ____ left **sleeve yoke stitches** onto the needle, place a marker. Slip ____ **front yoke stitches** onto the needle, place a marker. Slip ____ right **sleeve yoke stitches** onto the needle, and place a marker in a different color to mark the beginning of the yoke rounds. You should have ____ stitches (**total yoke stitches**).

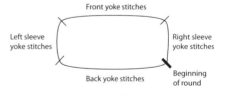

Front yoke stitches

Left sleeve yoke stitches

Right sleeve yoke stitches

Back yoke stitches

Beginning of round

7 Work border pattern on yoke

Work 2 rounds even. On the next round, increase or decrease if necessary to achieve a number of stitches that is an even multiple of your yoke pattern repeat (space the increases or decreases evenly on the round).

Note: Because of the way the raglan decreases affect the pattern, it's less critical to fit the pattern into a repeat sequence here than it is at the bottom of the sweater. It's more important to have your patterns centered on the four segments (two sleeves, front, and back).

Add the contrasting color and work the border pattern at the base of the yoke. When you have completed the pattern, cut the contrasting color, leaving an end long enough to secure later.

AT THE SAME TIME, when the yoke measures 1 inch (2.5 cm), begin the decrease sequence in step 8.

8 Work raglan decreases

On every other round, k2tog after each marker and ssk before each marker (decreasing a total of 8 stitches on the round). Maintain the consistency of your border pattern as you work the decreases.

See page 14 for tips on altering the yoke depth and the top of page 61 for ways to vary the placement, and appearance, of the decreases.

9 Knit optional short rows and neckband

Optional: If desired, you can work more short rows to raise the back neck when

the yoke measures 2 inches (5 cm) less than **yoke depth** (____ inches [cm]), or ____ inches (cm). *See "short-row shaping at the back neck" on page 29.*

Continuing established raglan decrease sequence, work until the yoke measures ____ inches (cm) (**yoke depth**) on the front.

If you reach ____ **neck stitches** before you reach the yoke depth, stop decreasing, work 1 or 2 rounds plain, and begin the neckband.

If you still have too many stitches for the neck when you reach the yoke depth, decrease evenly around on the next round to ____ **neck stitches** and then begin the neckband.

Work neckband in k2, p2 ribbing for 1 inch (2.5 cm), or desired height of neckband. Bind off loosely in pattern.

10 Finish

Join each underarm opening with a seam, three-needle bind-off, or kitchener stitch, as desired.

Weave in the ends.

Tips for raglan decreases (step 8)

The decrease line will form what looks like an angled "seam."

While you are working the border pattern, work the decreases and any "seam" stitches in the main color, stranding the contrasting color very loosely behind the seam so the fabric does not pucker.

If you would like a more decorative "seam" line, work the decreases 2 or 3 stitches before and after each marker, instead of placing the decreases right next to the markers. If you are not sure where you'd like to place the decreases, make a small swatch and test several options.

Lithuanian sheep

In the nineteenth and early twentieth centuries, the Lithuanian Coarsewool sheep was found on small farms around the country. Originally, there were several types of coarse-wool sheep in Lithuania, including both short-tail and long-tail varieties. The original long-tailed sheep had predominantly white fleeces; the short-tailed sheep grew darker wools. Like many native breeds, their fleeces were double-coated, consisting of both bristly guard hairs and a softer undercoat used to spin knitting and craft yarn. Today, these variant types have largely been interbred and wool colors vary from gray and black to brown and gray-brown.

In the middle of the twentieth century, the Lithuanian Black-Headed breed was established by combining the local coarse-wool sheep with British stock (sources indicate Shropshire and possibly Oxford Down infusions) and German black-headed meat sheep. Lithuanian Black-Headed sheep grow a white, moderately fine, single-coated fleece, with black only on the head, ears, and legs.

With the new European Union agricultural regulations, farming is difficult and often impossible for small farmers. The native sheep are on conservation status. Although there are only four flocks of Lithuanian Coarsewool sheep in existence, totaling around a hundred animals, their numbers appear to be growing, at least in part because they are resistant to many diseases and they can lamb twice a year. The Lithuanian Black-Headed sheep are also being intensively managed to conserve the genetic resources they represent.

Raglan Pullover with Multiple Patterns

This sweater is made in the same fashion as project 2 (page 50). The body of the sample sweater shown here is decorated with multiple pattern stitches, the sleeves have a matching border, and the yoke is worked in a solid color. You can work as many patterns as you like on this sweater, in any placement, and use several colors. Repeating some of the colors between the patterns will tie everything together for an attractive finished look. See page 73 for notes on fitting large patterns.

✔ Striped ribbing
✔ Play with color patterns: rearrange elements and invent variations
✔ Lower body and sleeves worked in the round to the underarm, then joined so the yoke can be worked in the round

The illustration shows a sweater with a 40-inch (102-cm) body circumference and 24-inch (61-cm) body length (including 2 inches [5 cm] of ribbing) in medium-weight yarn with 4¾ stitches and 7 rows to the inch (19 stitches and 28 rows to 10 cm).

I added a few one-round stripes at the bottom to lift the elk away from the ribbing,

put in two evergreen trees to fill the pattern at the sides, and included one-row stripes above the band in the yoke area to balance the weight of the patterning in the lower body of the sweater.

Patterns: Elk with extra trees (page 41), Entertaining Geometric Border (page 43), and a few plain stripes.

63

Get ready   *yarn & needles*

Yarn

This sweater can be made with any type of yarn. Wool or a wool blend will make a warm winter garment, while a sweater made of cotton can be worn in other seasons as well. As long as the yarn is smooth and comes in the colors you want, it will work well in this design.

Any weight of yarn will work, but for practice I suggest a medium-weight yarn and U.S. size 7 or 8 (4.5 or 5 mm) knitting needles.

Yarn guidelines, including a yardage estimate table, are on pages 20–22.

Knitting needles

In a size appropriate for the yarn you've chosen:

✦ Circular needle for body: for an adult sweater, use a needle at least 29 inches (74 cm) long

✦ Circular needle for sleeves and neckband: 16 inches (40 cm) long

✦ Double-pointed needles for cuffs: set of 4 or 5

Tip: Some knitters find that their gauge is more consistent if they knit the colorwork portions of a project on a needle that is one size larger than the needle they use for the solid areas. You may also prefer to use smaller needles (often two sizes smaller) when you work the ribbing on the body and the sleeve cuffs.

Needle guidelines, including tips on choosing lengths of circular needles and on working small tubes on circulars, are on pages 18–20.

Additional supplies

✦ Stitch markers
✦ Spare needle or stitch holders

Get set *stitches, gauge & size*

Stitches and gauge

1 Select the pattern stitches for your sweater. Use the combination shown in the illustration on page 63 or choose your own combination of stitches, either from this book or from a knitting-stitch library.

2 Make a gauge swatch in stockinette stitch.

Knit the swatch in the round to make sure you get an accurate gauge measurement. If you don't have a lot of experience with colorwork, make both a solid swatch and a colorwork swatch to see if you get the same gauge with the same size needle.

3 Measure your gauge. Write the stitch gauge and row gauge on the sweater-planning worksheet on page 67.

Size

1 Measure your favorite sweater or use the size charts on page 16 to determine the basic dimensions for your sweater. Write the measurements on the visual plan on page 66 and the sweater-planning worksheet on page 67.

2 Use the calculations on the worksheets on pages 67–69 to figure all the remaining numbers before you start, or just calculate each new number as you need it.

3 Transfer the resulting numbers to the visual plan on page 66 or the step-by-step instructions on pages 70–72, depending on how much guiding detail you would like to have while you knit.

Knit! *option I: using a visual plan*

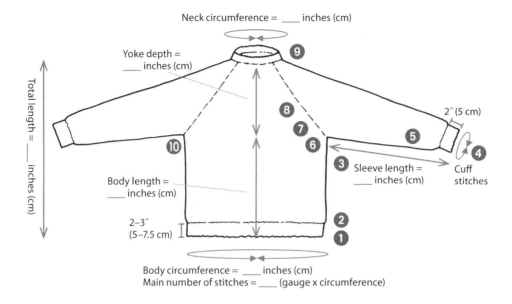

Neck circumference = _____ inches (cm)

Yoke depth = _____ inches (cm)

2″ (5 cm)

Total length = _____ inches (cm)

Sleeve length = _____ inches (cm)

Cuff stitches

Body length = _____ inches (cm)

2–3″ (5–7.5 cm)

Body circumference = _____ inches (cm)
Main number of stitches = _____ (gauge x circumference)

LOWER BODY

1 Cast on _____ stitches (stitches to cast on, or 90% of main number of stitches) and knit ribbing

2 Increase to _____ stitches (main number of stitches), change to stockinette stitch, and work border and body patterns

3 Work to body length and knit optional short rows

SLEEVES

4 Cast on _____ cuff stitches and knit ribbing

5 Work border at lower edge of sleeve; increase at even intervals along underarm to _____ sleeve stitches, then work even until sleeve reaches sleeve length

UPPER BODY

6 Join sleeves and body

7 Work yoke patterns;

8 Work raglan decreases every other round, and decrease to _____ neck stitches

FINISH

9 Work neckband and bind off

10 Join underarms and weave in ends

Knit! *option 2: using planning worksheets*   Lithuania
Sweater *with* Multiple Patterns

Measurements for project 3

	Calculation	Example	Description
Stitch gauge	____ stitches = 1 inch or 1 cm	**5** stitches = 1 inch	**Stitch gauge** is critical for knitting a sweater that fits properly.
Row gauge	____ rows = 1 inch or 1 cm	**6** rows = 1 inch	**Row gauge** is often important for raglan sweaters, because it can be used to calculate the placement of decreases. However, I prefer to fudge as I go!
Body width	____ inches (cm)	**20** inches	Measure the **width** of the sweater body.
Body circumference	____ x 2 = ____ inches (cm)	20 x 2 = **40** inches	Double the body width for the **circumference of the sweater**.
Total length	____ inches (cm)	**24** inches	Measure the **length** of the sweater body from cast-on to shoulder.
Sleeve length	____ inches (cm)	**18** inches	Measure the **sleeve length** from the cuff edge to the underarm.
Yoke depth	____ ÷ 2 = ____ inches (cm)	20 ÷ 2 = **10** inches	Divide the body width by 2 to calculate the **yoke depth**. (See tips on page 14 for altering yoke depth.)
Body length	____ – ____ = ____ inches (cm)	24 – 10 = **14** inches	Subtract the yoke depth from the total body length to calculate the **length of the body from the cast-on edge to the armhole.**
Upper sleeve circumference	____ x .40 = ____ inches (cm)	40 x .40 = **16** inches	Take 35 to 40 percent of the body circumference to calculate the **upper sleeve circumference**, depending on whether you want tighter (.35) or looser (.40) sleeves.
Neck circumference	____ inches (cm)	**14** inches	Measure the **circumference around the neck** or use the sweater proportions chart on page 14 to calculate the neck circumference.

Need a slightly different stitch count? Increase or decrease by a few.

A (beside Sleeve length row)
B (beside Yoke depth row)
C (beside Body length row)

Stitch counts for project 3

	Calculation	Example	Description
a Main number of stitches	___ x ___ = ___ stitches	40 x 5 = **200 stitches**	Multiply the body circumference by your stitch gauge to calculate the **main number of stitches**. Round this up or down as necessary to equal an even multiple of the pattern stitches you've chosen. (You can adjust your stitch count slightly between pattern bands.)
b Stitches to cast on	___ x .9 = ___ stitches	200 x .9 = **180 stitches** 180 stitches is a multiple of 4	Take 90 percent of the main number of stitches to calculate the **number of stitches to cast on**. Round up or down to a multiple of 4 stitches for working k2, p2 ribbing.
c Front stitches & Back stitches	___ ÷ 2 = ___ stitches	200 ÷ 2 = **100 stitches**	Divide the main number of stitches in half to determine the **number of stitches in the upper front and upper back.**
d Sleeve stitches	___ x ___ = ___ stitches	16 x 5 = **80 stitches**	Multiply the upper sleeve circumference by your stitch gauge to calculate the **number of sleeve stitches** required at the top of each sleeve.
e Underarm stitches	___ x 2 = ___ stitches	5 x 2 = **10 stitches**	Multiply your stitch gauge by 2 to calculate how many stitches to set aside for a 2-inch (5-cm) **underarm seam.** (Metric: Divide the number of stitches in 10 cm by 2 to reach the same number.)
f Front yoke stitches & Back yoke stitches	___ – ___ = ___ stitches	100 – 10 = **90 stitches**	Subtract the number of underarm stitches from the front/back stitches to calculate how many **stitches from the front and back** will remain for the **yoke**.

This example has been set up with numbers that happen to result in an adult's sweater with a finished chest measurement of 40″ (102 cm) that falls to just below the waistline. If you're not that size, and only a few of us will be, use the guidelines on pages 14–17 and measurements you gather for yourself to make a sweater that is customized for its wearer.

Stitch counts for project 3 (continued)

		Calculation	Example	Description
g	*Sleeve yoke stitches*	____ − ____ = ____ stitches	80 − 10 = **70** stitches	Subtract the number of underarm stitches from the sleeve stitches to calculate how many **stitches from each sleeve** will remain for the **yoke**.
h	*Total yoke stitches*	____ + ____ + ____ + ____ = ____ stitches	90 + 90 + 70 + 70 = **320** stitches	To determine the **total number of stitches at the beginning of the yoke**, add front yoke stitches, back yoke stitches, left sleeve yoke stitches, and right sleeve yoke stitches.
i	*Neck stitches*	____ x____ = ____ stitches	14 x 5 = **70** **68** stitches is a multiple of 4	Multiply the neck circumference by the stitch gauge to calculate the **neck stitches**, which represent the number of stitches that remain after the yoke decreasing. Round this up or down to a multiple of 4 for working k2, p2 ribbing.
j	*Cuff stitches*	____ stitches	**40** stitches 40 stitches is a multiple of 4	After you knit the body of your sweater, wrap the ribbing around your wrist and count the **number of stitches for the cuff**. For a rough estimate of this number, divide the main number of stitches by 5. Round up or down to a multiple of 4 for working k2, p2 ribbing

Need a slightly different stitch count? Increase or decrease by a few.

Knit! *option 3: a step-by-step project sheet*

Use this project sheet if you are not yet comfortable working directly from the sweater-planning diagram. With time, you'll find that you no longer need to refer to these instructions.

Do the calculations on the planning worksheets on pages 67–69 so you have the numbers to fill in here.

1 Cast on and knit ribbing

b
With a 29-inch (74-cm) circular needle and the contrasting color, cast on ____ stitches (**stitches to cast on**). Join, being careful not to twist, place a marker at the beginning of the round, and knit in the round.

Work in k2, p2 ribbing, adding main color and changing colors for stripes as desired (see striped ribbing on page 36), until the ribbing measures 2 or 3 inches (5 or 7.5 cm), or desired length.

2 Work patterns

a
Use the main color and stockinette stitch (knit every round). Increase to ____ stitches (**main number of stitches**) on the first round as follows: *K9, increase 1, repeat from * to end of round. (Fudge if you need a few extra stitches to achieve a multiple of your first pattern.)

c
c
On the next round, knit ____ **back stitches**, place a second marker, knit to the end of the round (____ **front**

stitches). You now have a marker at the beginning of the round and a second marker halfway around, marking the side "seams" of the sweater.

Work even in stockinette stitch in your chosen patterns, adding or dropping contrasting colors as needed. At the start and end of your colors, leave ends long enough to weave in later.

3 Work lower body and optional short rows

c
When you have completed your patterns, work even in the main color until body measures ____ inches (cm) (**body length**) from the cast-on edge.

Optional: See "short-row shaping for the body" on page 29.

e
On the next round, bind off or place on hold ____ **underarm stitches** at each side marker, with half of the underarm stitches coming before the marker and half after it. Remove the markers.

Set the body aside, placing its stitches on a spare needle or stitch holders.

4 Cast on and knit cuffs

j
Using double-pointed needles and contrasting color, cast on ____ stitches (**cuff stitches**). Join, being careful not to twist, place a marker at the beginning of the round, and knit in the round.

Work in k2, p2 ribbing, adding main color and changing colors for stripes as desired, until the cuff measures 2 inches (5 cm), or desired length.

⑤ Work sleeve increases

Add main color and change to stockinette stitch. Work the patterns as desired, adding and dropping contrasting colors as needed. At the start and end of your colors, leave ends long enough to weave in later. When you have completed your patterns, cut the contrasting colors and continue in stockinette with the main color.

AT THE SAME TIME, begin increasing for the sleeve as follows: On every 4th round, k1, increase 1, knit to just before last stitch, increase 1, k1.

When the stitches no longer fit comfortably on the double-pointed needles, change to the 16-inch (40-cm) circular needle.

Keep an eye on the shape of your sleeve and measure it against your model sweater or try your sleeve on after every few inches (cm) to make sure the sleeve is increasing at a comfortable rate. If your sleeve is becoming wide too quickly, start increasing every 6th round. If it is not widening quickly enough, start increasing every 3rd round.

d
A
Continue increasing until you have ____ **sleeve stitches** and then work even until sleeve is ____ inches (cm) (**sleeve length**) from the cast-on edge.

On the next round, bind off or place on hold ____ **underarm stitches** at the marker, with half of the underarm stitches coming before the marker and half after it. Remove the marker. **e**

Set the sleeve aside, placing its stitches on a spare needle or stitch holders.

Make second sleeve the same way as the first, steps 4 and 5.

⑥ Join sleeves and body

Arrange the body and sleeve stitches on one long circular needle, as follows: Slip ____ **back yoke stitches** onto the needle, place a marker. Slip ____ left **sleeve yoke stitches** onto the needle, place a marker. Slip ____ **front yoke stitches** onto the needle, place a marker. Slip ____ right **sleeve yoke stitches** onto the needle, and place a marker in a different color to mark the beginning of the yoke rounds. You should have ____ stitches (**total yoke stitches**). **f** **g** **f** **g** **h**

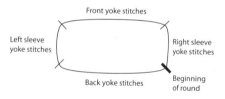

Front yoke stitches

Left sleeve yoke stitches

Right sleeve yoke stitches

Back yoke stitches

Beginning of round

⑦ Work yoke patterns and raglan decreases

Work 2 rounds even. On the next round, increase or decrease if necessary to achieve a number of stitches that is an even multiple of your yoke pattern repeat (space the increases or decreases evenly on the round).

Set up patterns.

Note: Because of the way the raglan decreases affect the pattern, it's less critical to fit the pattern into a repeat sequence here than it is at the bottom of the sweater. It's more important to have your patterns centered on the four segments (two sleeves, front, and back).

AT THE SAME TIME, when the yoke measures 1 inch (2.5 cm), begin the decrease sequence in step 8.

8 Work raglan decreases

On every other round, k2tog after each marker and ssk before each marker (decreasing a total of 8 stitches on the round). Maintain the consistency of your border pattern as you work the decreases, then change to a solid color to work the rest of the yoke.

See page 14 for tips on altering the yoke depth and page 61 for ways to vary the placement, and appearance, of the decreases.

9 Knit optional short rows and neckband

Optional: If desired, you can work more short rows to raise the back neck when

the yoke measures 2 inches (5 cm) less than **yoke depth** (___ inches [cm]), or ___ inches (cm). *See "short-row shaping at the back neck" on page 29.*   **B**

Continuing established raglan decrease sequence, work until the yoke measures ___ inches (cm) (**yoke depth**) on the front.   **B**

If you reach ___ **neck stitches** before you reach the yoke depth, stop decreasing, work 1 or 2 rounds plain, and begin the neckband.   **i**

If you still have too many stitches for the neck when you reach the yoke depth, decrease evenly around on the next round to ___ **neck stitches** and then begin the neckband.   **i**

Work neckband in k2, p2 ribbing for 1 inch (2.5 cm), or desired height of neckband. Bind off loosely in pattern.

10 Finish

Join each underarm opening with a seam, three-needle bind-off, or kitchener stitch, as desired.

Weave in the ends.

Working with large motifs

Large motifs can be both challenging and rewarding. The first step is to figure out how big the motif is, and how it will fit into the pieces that you are knitting at your gauge. Remember to give the motif some breathing space!

Here are three ideas for ways to use the Lily motif (page 40) on different types of raglan sweaters at a variety of gauges. All of the sweaters are the 40-inch (102-cm) circumference used for most of the examples in this book.

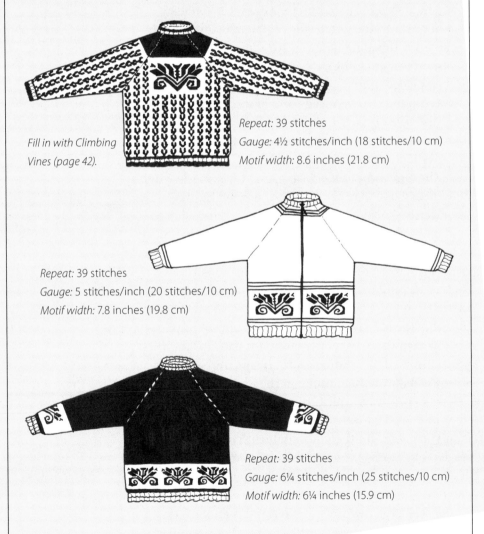

Fill in with Climbing Vines (page 42).

Repeat: 39 stitches
Gauge: 4½ stitches/inch (18 stitches/10 cm)
Motif width: 8.6 inches (21.8 cm)

Repeat: 39 stitches
Gauge: 5 stitches/inch (20 stitches/10 cm)
Motif width: 7.8 inches (19.8 cm)

Repeat: 39 stitches
Gauge: 6¼ stitches/inch (25 stitches/10 cm)
Motif width: 6¼ inches (15.9 cm)

Iceland

Knitting was introduced to Iceland toward the end of the Middle Ages, most likely by the Dutch. A woolen mitten, a pair of socks, and several scraps of knitted fabric found in southern Iceland date from the sixteenth century, and in 1582 and 1583 a bishop in northern Iceland recorded that tenant farmers paid him rent in knitted goods.

After its introduction to the region, knitting quickly became a national industry. In 1624, more than seventy thousand pairs of mittens were exported. By 1743, exports included more than one hundred thousand pairs of mittens and two hundred pairs of stockings. Sweaters were also sold abroad, and the numbers of hand-knitted items made in, and sent away from, Iceland continued to grow well into the nineteenth century.

At the same time, underwear, jackets, accessories, and household items were also made for personal and religious use. Because knitting was both an industry and a home craft, men and women alike knitted during this period.

The earliest Icelandic sweaters were women's knitted jackets and men's vests. Written patterns for sweaters, socks, caps, and underwear were used in Iceland as early as 1760, but knitting terms have changed so much since then that the old-style instructions are almost impossible to decipher. Charts were used for patterns for fine-gauge insoles (fabric linings worn inside thin women's shoes) and mittens beginning in the nineteenth century. Before then, knitters must have made up their own designs or copied patterns from items worn by friends or family members. In the mid-nineteenth century, modern-looking cardigans knitted out of two natural colors of wool at a loose gauge of 3½ stitches per inch became popular.

The yoke-style sweaters that Iceland is famous for today were not developed until the twentieth century.

During the 1940s and early '50s, Icelandic knitters made drop-shoulder sweaters with patterns on the upper body and the lower. In the 1950s and '60s, circular sweaters with patterned yokes exploded onto the fashion scene. They have maintained their appeal ever since. Based on traditional Scandinavian designs, these sweaters are sometimes knitted with traditional colorwork patterns, but are just as likely to be made with patterns created by individual knitters and professional designers.

The yarn used is often natural-colored wool. Traditional Icelandic yarn or fluffy lopi (unspun fiber; see the box on the next page) is characteristic of the style, but the patterns are also beautiful in modern singles yarns (unplied yarns) that are readily available in worsted and bulky weights. The sweater body is normally knitted in a solid color or a very simple color pattern, with more detailed colorwork designs used on the yoke and as bands on the sleeves and lower body.

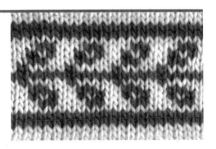

CHAPTER 4 HIGHLIGHTS

Skills
☑ Color patterning in circular bands

Techniques
☑ Knitting with unspun lopi yarn
☑ Fitting patterns on a yoke

Garment styling
☑ All pieces worked in the round
☑ Circular-yoke construction
☑ Pullover or cardigan

Techniques

Knitting with unspun lopi yarn

Knitting with lopi is very much like knitting with regular yarn. Once the knitting has been completed, the structure of the stitches and fabric gives strength to the fabric. Before it is knitted, however, lopi is very fragile and will tear easily. Weave in your ends as you go so they don't fray.

When sewing seams, it is best to use a stronger yarn in a matching color. This will ensure that the seams won't split open in the future.

Fitting patterns on a yoke

There are two ways to work color patterns on the yokes of Icelandic sweaters. You can work horizontal pattern bands or a full-yoke pattern, which needs to be designed to fit the individual sweater. I'll introduce you to both,

The story of lopi yarn

Lopi is unspun fiber that has been pulled out, or drafted, into long strands and wound into flat bundles, called *plates*.

The term *lopi* originally referred to thick strands of wool from Icelandic sheep in an early stage of fiber preparation, but later came to refer to strands of wool that were almost as thin as knitting yarn but contained very little twist. When woolen mills were first introduced to Iceland, farmers would send fleece to the mill, where it would be cleaned and prepared for spinning. The actual spinning was done on home spinning wheels.

In 1920, Elín Guðjónsdóttir Snæhólm used a knitting machine to make her husband a scarf from unspun lopi, skipping the step of spinning the fiber into a true yarn. She wrote about her experience in an article published in *Hlín*, a popular women's publication about crafts. Other busy women found this shortcut appealing and the use of unspun fiber caught on quickly for machine knitters. For some reason, about ten years passed before hand knitters started using the unspun lopi in sweaters.

Not everything that is sold under the name "lopi" really is, either in fiber content or preparation. Modern yarns called lopi have often been lightly spun.

with detailed information on working with horizontal pattern bands. If you are interested in full-yoke patterning, I suggest that you experiment with the horizontal bands enough to understand the basic yoke structure and then start experimenting with custom designing.

Horizontal pattern bands

In the first method, small horizontal pattern stitches are used. Decrease rounds can be worked on plain rounds between the bands.

You will have to adjust the number of stitches in the yoke to work with the multiple used in each pattern. For example, if you are working with a chart that has a 12-stitch repeat, you need a total number of stitches that is a multiple of 12, such as 216, 240, or 252. When you change to a pattern stitch with a different repeat, fudge the number of decreases made in one of the decrease rounds to get the correct multiple for the new pattern.

Within the sweater patterns, step 6 includes the yoke decreases. Here is a detailed walk-through of how to coordinate the bands with the decrease rounds, using the patterns in the sample sweater on page 93 (shown smaller on page 76) and the measurements and gauge calculations on the sample worksheets just as reference points. The numbers are included here so you can follow the discussion without having to refer back and forth.

When you plan your own sweaters, remember that the placement of the decrease rounds is not set in stone—get them in about the right places, as you'll see in this example, and you'll come out fine.

The sample sweater is designed at 4¾ stitches and 6¾ rows to the inch (19 stitches and 27 rows to 10 cm). It has a 40-inch (102-cm) circumference and other measurements as in the chart on page 97. The yoke is 10 inches (25.4 cm) deep and there are 302 total yoke stitches.

The first decrease round will be worked at about half the yoke depth, or when the yoke is about 5 inches (12.7 cm) deep.

The first pattern is the Playful Geometric Pattern, with a repeat of 12 stitches by 12 rounds. The closest multiple (25 repeats) is 300 stitches. Two stitches are

① Playful Geometric
    Pattern
② Line of Trees,
    light-on-dark
③ Mirrored Trees,
    light-on-dark

Playful Geometric
Pattern

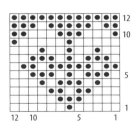

decreased out (probably at the middle of each sleeve) on a plain round before the patterning begins.

After the first band has been completed, the yoke is about 2 inches (5 cm) deep; it's not time for a decrease round yet.

The second pattern is the Line of Trees, with a repeat of 6 stitches by 11 rounds. It's worked light-on-dark, instead of dark-on-light. It fits into 300 stitches evenly (50 repeats). Because it's good to have some spacing between bands, this pattern begins after 4 rounds of the new background color.

At the end of this sequence, the yoke is about 4¼ inches (11 cm) deep. It's easiest just to measure, but if you want to calculate here are the numbers: 2 rounds plain + 12 rounds pattern 1 + 4 rounds plain + 11 rounds pattern 2 = 29 rounds. At 6¾ rounds to the inch, 29 rounds is 4⅓ inches; at 27 rounds to 10 cm, it's 10.8 cm.

It's almost time for a decrease round, as well as 4 rounds between patterns. The decrease round would work well on the third or fourth of those 4 rounds; 200 stitches remain.

The third pattern is Mirrored Trees, with a repeat of 8 stitches by 15 rounds, again worked light-on-dark. It fits into 200 stitches evenly (25 repeats).

When it has been completed, the yoke is about 7 inches (18 cm) deep. This measurement is between ⅔ and ¾ of the yoke depth (between 6.6 and 7.5 inches, or 16.5 and 19 cm). It's time for the second decrease round. If you want to calculate: 29 previous rounds + 4 plain + 15 pattern 3 = 48 rounds. At 6¾ rounds to the inch, 48 rounds is just over 7 inches; at 27 rounds to 10 cm, it's 17.8 cm.

It's also close to 1 to 2 inches (2.5 to 5 cm) less than the full yoke depth. The remaining rounds can be worked plain, either with or without short-row shaping, or another narrow pattern band might be fitted in.

In the sample sweater, there's no extra band. The final rounds are worked plain, followed by the neckline decreases and ribbing, all worked in the dark background color.

The important lesson here? Fudge!

Line of Trees

Dark-on-light.

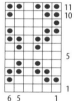

Light-on-dark.

Mirrored Trees

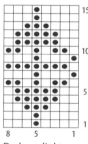

Dark-on-light.

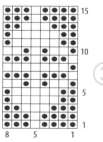

Light-on-dark.

Full-yoke pattern

In books or magazines, you may have seen yoke patterns with charts for the entire yoke all in one. These charts are custom-designed for each sweater, to fit the sizes and colors chosen by the designer.

The bottom of the chart begins with a repeat that fits evenly into the number of stitches that are on the needles after the sleeves and body have been joined at the base of the yoke. The top of the chart ends with a repeat that fits evenly into the number of stitches that will remain for the neck. The decreases are built into the chart, flowing along with the pattern, instead of being worked in plain rounds between bands.

After you've made a few yoke sweaters with horizontal bands, you may find yourself with the curiosity and confidence to experiment with this type of design. I've given two examples to show how the idea works.

A chart for a full-yoke pattern incorporates the decreases within the pattern itself. It needs to be individually designed for a specific size and gauge of sweater. Once you have experience working with pattern bands, you may find yourself coming up with full-yoke pattern ideas.

These patterns will fit a yoke that is about 40 rounds deep, because you would want a few plain rounds at the top and bottom. They require that the total yoke stitches (when sleeves and body have been joined) be divisible by 12.

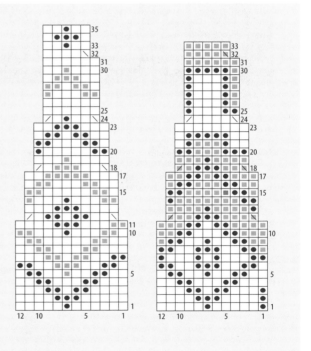

Pattern stitches

Alternating Geometric Pattern

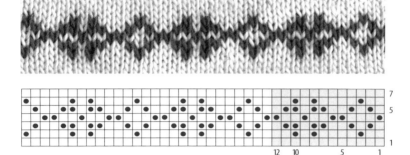

Repeat:
12 stitches
by 7 rows

Branch with Leaves

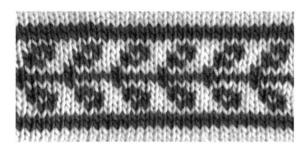

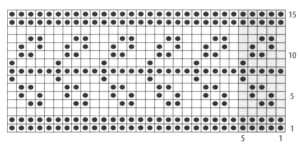

Repeat:
5 stitches
by 15 rows

The names on these patterns are not traditional.

Zigzags and Stars

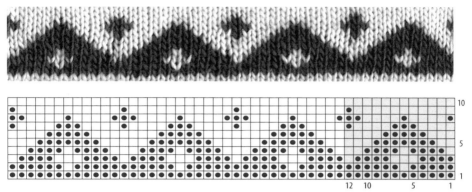

Repeat: 12 stitches by 10 rows

Offset Reflection

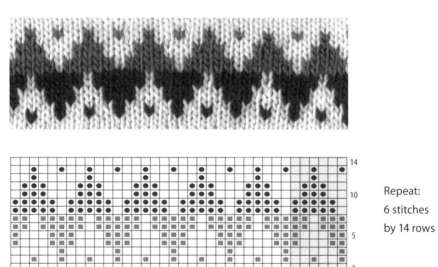

Repeat:
6 stitches
by 14 rows

See page 91 for variations on the Offset Reflection pattern.

Line of Trees

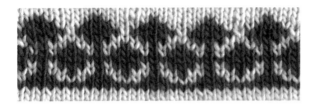

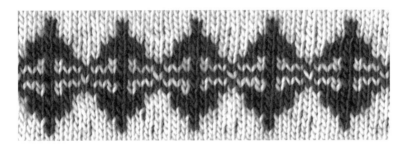

Repeat:
6 stitches
by 11 rows

Mirrored Trees

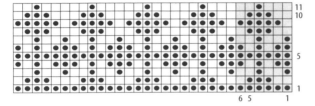

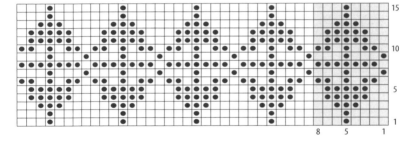

Repeat:
8 stitches
by 15 rows

Small Checks, Positive and Negative

This chart is intended to be worked as a band on the Icelandic-style garments, but you can also use it as an overall pattern on a simple sweater shape.

The two charts show how to modify a pattern to fit in a smaller area: 3 × 3 squares change to 2 × 2 squares.

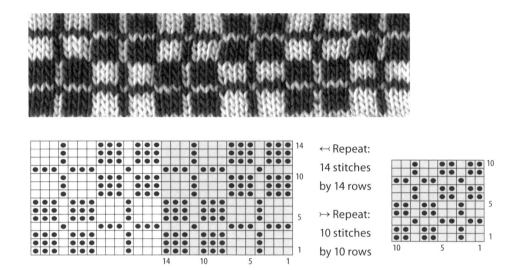

↤ Repeat:
14 stitches
by 14 rows

↦ Repeat:
10 stitches
by 10 rows

Playful Geometric Pattern

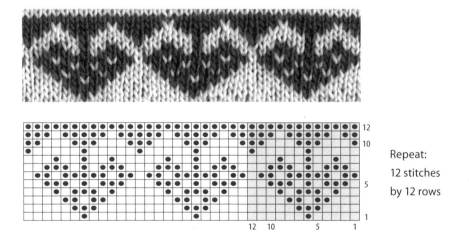

Repeat:
12 stitches
by 12 rows

Capelet

This stylish capelet will let you practice working the yoke decreases that are used on a sweater without knitting the sweater body or sleeves. Because this is essentially a sweater yoke, it is intended to be short: a capelet, rather than a cape. It works up very quickly if you use chunky yarn.

✅ *Color patterns worked in bands, in the round*
✅ *Shape with decreases worked between the pattern bands*

The illustration shows two capelets, one for an adult and one for a child, worked in chunky-weight yarn with 3¼ stitches and 4½ rows to the inch (13 stitches and 18 rows to 10 cm).

The adult's has a 60-inch (152-cm) lower circumference, a 14-inch (36-cm) length, and an 18-inch (46-cm) neck opening with a 1-inch (2.5-cm) ribbing finish. The child's has a 40-inch (102-cm) lower circumference, a 10-inch (25.4-cm) length, and a 14-inch (36-cm) neck opening with a turtleneck finish.

The charts were modified to fit within the smaller area of the child's garment: the 3-stitch squares in the lower band became 2-stitch squares, and on the center pattern only the lower half of the vertical repeat was used.

Patterns for adult's capelet: Small Checks (page 83), Mirrored Trees (page 82), and Zigzags and Stars (page 81).

Patterns for child's capelet: Small Checks modified (page 83), Mirrored Trees lower half (page 82), and Alternating Geometric Pattern (page 80).

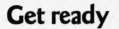
Get ready   *yarn & needles*

Iceland
Capelet

Yarn

Smooth yarn will show off color patterns best. Unspun lopi wool will give you the feeling that you're knitting a real Icelandic garment, but just about any type of yarn will work for this design.

For practice I suggest a chunky-weight yarn and U.S. size 9 or 10 (5.5 or 6 mm) knitting needles. You will need a total of approximately 500 yards (460 m) of chunky-weight yarn.

Knitting needles

In a size appropriate for the yarn you've chosen:

✧ Circular needle: 24 to 29 inches (60 to 74 cm) long

✧ Circular needle: 12 to 16 inches (30 to 40 cm) long

Two sizes smaller than primary needles—for neckband or collar, choose one of these:

✧ Double-pointed needles: set of 4 or 5

✧ Circular needle: 12 to 16 inches (30 to 40 cm) long

Tip: Some knitters find that their gauge is more consistent if they knit the colorwork portions of a project on a needle that is one size larger than the needle they use for the solid areas. You may also prefer to use smaller needles (often two sizes smaller) when you work the ribbing on the body and the sleeve cuffs.

Needle guidelines, including tips on choosing lengths of circular needles and on working small tubes on circulars, are on pages 18–20.

Additional supply

✧ Stitch marker

Get set *stitches, gauge & size*

Stitches and gauge

1 Select the pattern stitches for your capelet. Use one of the combinations shown on the sample illustrations (page 85), or choose your own combination of stitches from this book or from a knitting-stitch library.

2 Make a gauge swatch in stockinette stitch.

Knit the swatch in the round to make sure you get an accurate gauge measurement. If you don't have a lot of experience with colorwork, make both a solid swatch and a colorwork swatch to see if you get the same gauge with the same size needle.

It is a good idea to practice each pattern stitch to make sure you enjoy knitting it and to learn the pattern. That way you'll make any mistakes on your practice swatch instead of on your garment.

3 Measure your gauge and record it on the planning worksheet on page 89.

Size

1 Choose a size for your capelet and write the measurements on the visual plan on page 88 and in the boxes on the planning worksheet on page 89.

☆ Child: approximately 8–10 inches (20–25 cm) long, 40-inch (102-cm) circumference at lower edge, 14 inches (36 cm) at neck

☆ Adult: approximately 12–14 inches (30.5–35.5 cm) long, 60-inch (152-cm) circumference at lower edge, 18 inches (46 cm) at neck

Note: If you make the capelet much longer than I've specified, you will also need to make the circumference larger at the lower edge or the finished garment may be too tight at the bottom edge. You will also need to add an extra decrease round.

2 Use the calculations on the worksheet on page 89 to figure the remaining numbers before you start, or just calculate each new number as you need it.

3 Transfer the resulting numbers to the visual plan on page 88 or the step-by-step instructions on page 90, depending on how much guiding detail you would like to have while you knit. The visual plan can be helpful even if you are using the step-by-step project sheet as a confidence builder.

Knit! *option I: using a visual plan*

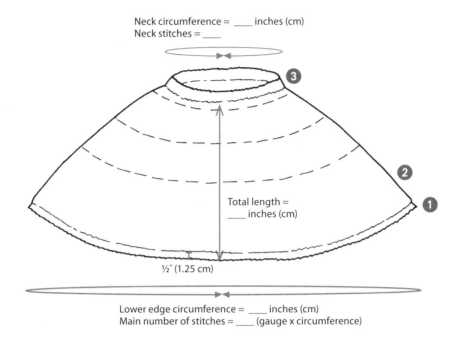

Neck circumference = ____ inches (cm)
Neck stitches = ____

Total length =
____ inches (cm)

½″ (1.25 cm)

Lower edge circumference = ____ inches (cm)
Main number of stitches = ____ (gauge x circumference)

1 Cast on ____ stitches (main number of stitches) and knit ribbing

2 Length of body is ____ inches (cm) from the cast-on edge. Work horizontal charted bands, decreasing between pattern areas as follows:

★ At ½ length, (k2, k2tog) around (fudge so you have the correct number for the pattern repeat of your next band)

★ At ¾ length, (k1, k2tog) around (fudge so you have the correct number for the pattern repeat of your next band)

★ At full length, (k1, k2tog, k2tog) around, fudging a little if necessary so you don't decrease past ____ stitches (neck stitches)

3 Work neckband and bind off

Knit! *option 2: using planning worksheets*

Iceland
Capelet

Measurements and stitch counts for project 4

	Calculation	Example	Description
Stitch gauge	____ stitches = 1 inch or 1 cm	**3½ stitches =** 1 inch	**Stitch gauge** is critical to getting a good fit.
Row gauge	____ stitches = 1 inch or 1 cm	**4 stitches =** 1 inch	**Row gauge** is not critical for this capelet, because you measure as you go and work decreases at the designated measurements. Row gauge may help you determine whether a specific pattern will fit in the next area that you will work.
Circumference at lower edge	____ inches (cm)	**60** inches	Desired **circumference of capelet at lower edge**.
Circumference at neck	____ inches (cm)	**18** inches	Desired **circumference of capelet at neck**.
Total length	____ inches (cm)	**12** inches	Approximate desired **total length** from lower edge (cast-on) to neck.
Main number of stitches	____ x ____ = ____ stitches	60 x 3½ = **210 stitches**	Multiply the circumference at the lower edge by your stitch gauge to calculate the **main number of stitches**. Round up or down to the closest multiple of the stitch repeat of your first horizontal pattern band.
Neck stitches	____ x ____ = ____ stitches	18 x 3½ = **63 stitches**	Multiply the circumference at the neck by your stitch gauge to calculate the **number of neck stitches**.
		64 stitches	Round up or down to the closest multiple of your ribbing repeat.

Keep in mind that you will want your main number of stitches to be a multiple of your pattern stitches, and that you may need to adjust the stitch count slightly between patterns. See pages 77–78.

Knit! *option 3: a step-by-step project sheet* — Iceland Capelet

Do the calculations on the planning worksheet on page 89 so you have the numbers to fill in here.

1 Cast on and work ribbing

With the larger needle and one of the contrasting colors, cast on ____ stitches (**main number of stitches**). Join, being careful not to twist, place a marker at the beginning of the round, and knit in the round.

Work in ribbing of your choice until the ribbing measures ½ inch (1.25 cm), or desired length.

2 Work pattern bands and decreases

Add the main color. Using both main and contrasting colors, follow the first chart of your choice to set up the first pattern, placing markers, if desired, between repeats.

Change patterns when you would like to. Adjust the stitch count as necessary when you begin a new pattern (see pages 77–78).

Work the decreases as follows, changing to the shorter circular needle when you need to:

Decrease round 1: Work even in first pattern until capelet measures approximately ½ of total length: ____ inches (cm) (.5 × ____ **total length**). Then, on a plain

round, work (k2, k2tog) around. *Fudge as necessary to reach an even multiple of your next pattern stitch.*

Decrease round 2: Work even in second pattern until capelet measures approximately ⅔ to ¾ of total length: ____ inches (cm) (.66 to .75 × ____ **total length**). Then, on a plain round, work (k1, k2tog) around. *Fudge as necessary to reach an even multiple of your next pattern stitch.*

Decrease round 3: Work even in third pattern until capelet measures approximately **total length**, or ____ inches (cm). Then, on a plain round, work (k1, k2tog, k2tog) around. Fudge a little if necessary so you do not decrease past ____ stitches (**neck stitches**).

3 Work neckband and finish

Cut all but one contrasting color and change to smaller needles. If necessary, decrease on the next round to ____ stitches (**neck stitches**).

Work neckband in ribbing of your choice for ½ to 1 inch (1.25 to 2.5 cm) for a crew neck or for 6 to 8 inches (15 to 20 cm) for a turtleneck. If you would like an open collar on your capelet, work the neckband back and forth, with the rows starting and ending at the center front.

Bind off very loosely in ribbing.

Weave in the ends.

Tweaking patterns

One of the most fun parts of designing your own sweaters is tweaking charts and pattern stitches to suit your own design. I've done this several times for the projects in this book, and my examples should give you some ideas for playing with patterns on your own. You can easily draw new charts on graph paper, or color squares in a spreadsheet on your computer, or use special knitting-chart software.

For the example of a Raglan Pullover with Multiple Patterns on page 63, I used a large chart that didn't fit evenly into the number of stitches I needed. The pattern is made up of large elk and smaller trees. Instead of fretting (or cutting a elk in half to make the pattern fit), I added extra tree motifs to the sides of the pattern to center it on the sweater body. You can also center large patterns on the body of a sweater by adding a very small pattern of checks or vertical stripes on the sides of the body, extending from the top of the ribbing to the underarms. This can also produce a slimming look for those of us who are concerned with such things!

For the capelet on page 85, I used two versions of the same chart concept for different-sized garments. For the woman's capelet, I used a 3×3 check pattern. For the child's version, I felt that this pattern would be too bold, so I reduced the checks to 2×2, for a more delicate feel. On the child's size, I also only worked the first few rows of the Mirrored Trees motif that I had used on the adult capelet, because I didn't have room for the whole pattern.

If you find a pattern you like but it doesn't seem exactly right for your design, try your hand at making your own tweaks. You can change the number of colors used, make the repeat larger or smaller (this is especially easy with geometric patterns), and even add new elements, such as small diamonds, crosses, or lines between and around the main motifs, to completely change the look.

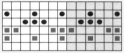
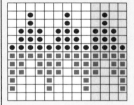
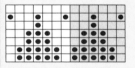

These are all variations on the Offset Reflection pattern (page 81), producing changes in horizontal and vertical repeats.

Pullover with Horizontal Bands on Yoke

This sweater yoke is decorated with three different charts. Each section of the yoke is knitted without decreases. A few plain rows worked between the charts allow you to decrease without interrupting the stitch pattern.

You can work all of the yoke sections with the same colors for a classic design, or change colors in each section for a more fanciful look.

✔ Color patterns in bands on yoke only
✔ Lower body and sleeves worked in the round to the armholes, then joined so the yoke can also be worked in the round
✔ Yoke decreases are worked between pattern bands
✔ Finishing? Just sew two short seams at the underarms!

The example shows a sweater with a 40-inch (102-cm) bust circumference and 18-inch (46-cm) body length (including 2 inches [5 cm] of welt) in worsted-weight yarn with 4¾ stitches and 6¾ rows to the inch (19 stitches and 27 rows to 10 cm).

See pages 77–78 for an explanation of how the patterns were planned.

Patterns: Mirrored Trees and Line of Trees (both page 82), and Playful Geometric Pattern (page 83).

Get ready   *yarn & needles*

Yarn

This sweater can be made with any type of yarn. Wool or a wool blend will make a warm winter garment, while a sweater made of cotton can be worn in other seasons as well. As long as the yarn is smooth and comes in the colors you want, it will work well in this design.

Any weight of yarn will work, but for practice I suggest a medium-weight yarn and U.S. size 7 or 8 (4.5 or 5 mm) knitting needles.

Yarn guidelines, including a yardage estimate table, are on pages 20–22.

Knitting needles

In a size appropriate for the yarn you've chosen:

✧ Circular needle for body: for an adult sweater, use a needle at least 29 inches (74 cm) long

✧ Circular needle for sleeves and neckband: 16 inches (40 cm) long

✧ Double-pointed needles for cuffs: set of 4 or 5

Tip: Some knitters find that their gauge is more consistent if they knit the colorwork portions of a project on a needle that is one size larger than the needle they use for the solid areas. You may also prefer to use smaller needles (often two sizes smaller) when you work the ribbing on the body and the sleeve cuffs.

Needle guidelines, including tips on choosing lengths of circular needles and on working small tubes on circulars, are on pages 18–20.

Additional supplies

✧ Stitch markers
✧ Spare needle or stitch holders

Get set *stitches, gauge & size*

Iceland
Sweater *with* Horizontal Bands

Stitches and gauge

1 Select the pattern stitches for your sweater. Use the combination shown in the illustration on page 93 or choose your own combination of stitches, either from this book or from a knitting-stitch library.

2 Make a gauge swatch in stockinette stitch.

Knit the swatch in the round to make sure you get an accurate gauge measurement. If you don't have a lot of experience with colorwork, make both a solid swatch and a colorwork swatch to see if you get the same gauge with the same size needle.

3 Measure your gauge. Write the stitch gauge and row gauge on the sweater-planning worksheet on page 97.

Size

1 Measure your favorite sweater or use the size charts on page 16 to determine the basic dimensions for your sweater. Write the measurements on the visual plan on page 96 and the sweater-planning worksheet on page 97.

2 Use the calculations on the worksheets on pages 97–99 to figure all the remaining numbers before you start, or just calculate each new number as you need it.

3 Transfer the resulting numbers to the visual plan on page 96 or the step-by-step instructions on pages 99–101, depending on how much guiding detail you would like to have while you knit.

Knit! *option I: using a visual plan*

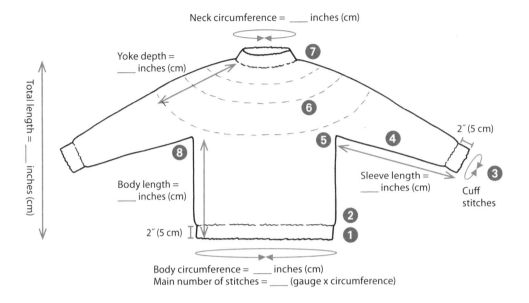

Neck circumference = _____ inches (cm)

Yoke depth = _____ inches (cm)

Total length = _____ inches (cm)

2˝ (5 cm)

Sleeve length = _____ inches (cm)

Cuff stitches

Body length = _____ inches (cm)

2˝ (5 cm)

Body circumference = _____ inches (cm)
Main number of stitches = _____ (gauge x circumference)

LOWER BODY

1 Cast on _____ stitches (90% of main number of stitches) and knit ribbing

2 Increase to _____ stitches (main number of stitches), change to stockinette stitch, and work to body length, knitting optional short rows if desired

SLEEVES

3 Cast on _____ cuff stitches and knit ribbing

4 Change to stockinette stitch and work sleeve; increase at even intervals along underarm to _____ sleeve stitches, then work even until sleeve reaches sleeve length

UPPER BODY

5 Join sleeves and body

6 Work patterns bands in yoke, decreasing on plain rounds as follows:

★ At ½ length, (k2, k2tog) around

★ At ⅔ to ¾ length, (k1, k2tog) around

★ At full length, (k1, k2tog, k2tog) around

FINISH

7 Work optional short rows and neckband and bind off

8 Join underarms and weave in ends

Knit! *option 2: using planning worksheets*

Iceland
Sweater *with* Horizontal Bands

Measurements for project 5

	Calculation	Example	Description
Stitch gauge	____ stitches = 1 inch or 1 cm	**4¾ stitches =** 1 inch	**Stitch gauge** is critical for knitting a sweater that fits properly.
Row gauge	____ rows = 1 inch or 1 cm	**6¾ rows =** 1 inch	**Row gauge** is not critical for this sweater, because you measure the yoke as you go and work decreases at the designated measurements. It may help you determine whether a specific pattern will fit in the next area that you will work.
Body width	____ inches (cm)	**20** inches	Measure the **width** of the sweater body.
Body circumference	____ x 2 = ____ inches (cm)	20 x 2 = **40** inches	Double the body width for the **circumference of the sweater**.
Total length	____ inches (cm)	**24** inches	Measure the **length** of the sweater body from cast-on to shoulder.
Yoke depth	____ ÷ 4 = ____ inches (cm)	40 ÷ 4 = **10** inches	Measure the **yoke depth** or use the sweater proportions chart on page 14 to calculate the yoke depth. (See tips on page 14 for altering yoke depth.)
Body length	____ – ____ = ____ inches (cm)	24 – 10 = **14** inches	Subtract the yoke depth from the total body length to calculate the **length of the body from the cast-on edge to the armhole.**
Sleeve length	____ inches (cm)	**18** inches	Measure the **sleeve length** from the cuff edge to the underarm.
Upper sleeve circumference	____ x .40 = ____ inches (cm)	40 x .40 = **16** inches	Take 35 to 40 percent of the body circumference to calculate the **upper sleeve circumference**, depending on whether you want tighter (.35) or looser (.40) sleeves.
Neck circumference	____ inches (cm)	**16** inches	Measure the **circumference around the neck** or use the sweater proportions chart on page 14 to calculate the neck circumference.

Stitch counts for project 5

	Calculation	Example	Description
a Main number of stitches	___ x ___ = ___ stitches	40 x 4.75 = **190** stitches	Multiply the body circumference by your stitch gauge to calculate the **main number of stitches**. *Note:* If you will be using a pattern in the lower body, round this up or down as necessary to equal an even multiple of the first pattern stitch you've chosen. (You can adjust your stitch count slightly between pattern bands.)
b Stitches to cast on	___ x .9 = ___ stitches	190 x .9 = **171** **172** stitches is a multiple of 2 and 4	Take 90 percent of the main number of stitches to calculate the **number of stitches to cast on**. Round up or down to the nearest multiple of your chosen ribbing.
c Front stitches & Back stitches	___ ÷ 2 = ___ stitches	190 ÷ 2 = **95** stitches	Divide the main number of stitches in half to determine the **number of stitches in the upper front and upper back.**
d Sleeve stitches	___ x ___ = ___ stitches	16 x 4.75 = **76** stitches	Multiply the upper sleeve circumference by your stitch gauge to calculate the **number of sleeve stitches** required at the top of the sleeve.
e Underarm stitches	___ x 2 = ___ stitches	4.75 x 2 = **9.5** **10** stitches is a nearby even number	Multiply your stitch gauge by 2 to calculate how many stitches to set aside for a 2-inch (5-cm) **underarm seam.** (Metric: Divide the number of stitches in 10 cm by 2 to reach the same number.) Round up or down to an even number.
f Front yoke stitches & Back yoke stitches	___ – ___ = ___ stitches	95 – 10 = **85** stitches	Subtract the number of underarm stitches from the front/back stitches to calculate how many **stitches from the front and back** will remain for the **yoke**.
g Sleeve yoke stitches	___ – ___ = ___ stitches	76 – 10 = **66** stitches	Subtract the number of underarm stitches from the sleeve stitches to calculate how many **stitches from each sleeve** will remain for the **yoke**.

This example has been set up with numbers that happen to result in an adult's sweater with a finished chest measurement of 40″ (102 cm) that falls to just below the waistline. If you're not that size, and only a few of us will be, use the guidelines on pages 14–17 and measurements you gather for yourself to make a sweater that is customized for its wearer.

Stitch counts for project 5 (continued)

	Calculation	Example	Description
h *Total yoke stitches*	___ + ___ + ___ + ___ = ___ stitches	85 + 85 + 66 + 66 = **302** stitches	To determine the **total number of stitches at the beginning of the yoke**, add the front yoke stitches, the back yoke stitches, the left sleeve yoke stitches, and the right sleeve yoke stitches.
i *Neck stitches*	___ x ___ = ___ stitches	16 x 4.75 = **76** **76** stitches is a multiple of 2 and of 4	Multiply the neck circumference by the stitch gauge to calculate the **neck stitches**, which represent the number of stitches that remain after the yoke decreasing. Round this up or down to a multiple of your chosen ribbing pattern.
j *Cuff stitches*	___ stitches	Wrap your wrist, or: 190 ÷ 5 = **38** stitches 38 stitches is a multiple of 2; 40 stitches is a multiple of 2 and 4	After you knit the body of your sweater, wrap the ribbing around your wrist and count the **number of stitches for the cuff**. For a rough estimate of this number, divide the main number of stitches by 5. Round up or down to a multiple of your chosen ribbing.

Need a slightly different stitch count? Increase or decrease by a few.

Knit! *option 3: a step-by-step project sheet* Iceland Sweater *with* Horizontal Bands

Use this project sheet if you are not yet comfortable working directly from the sweater-planning diagram. With time, you'll find that you no longer need to refer to these instructions.

Do the calculations on the planning worksheets on pages 97–99 so you have the numbers to fill in here.

① Cast on and knit ribbing

With a 29-inch (74-cm) circular needle and the main color, cast on ___ stitches (**stitches to cast on**). Join, being careful not to twist, place a marker at the beginning of the round, and knit in the round.

Work in your choice of ribbing until the ribbing measures 2 inches (5 cm), or desired length.

② Work lower body and optional short rows

Change to stockinette stitch (knit every round). Increase to ___ stitches (**main number of stitches**) on the first round as follows: *K9, increase 1, repeat from * to end of round. (Fudge a little if nec-

essary to reach your main number of stitches.)

 Work even in stockinette stitch until body measures ____ inches (cm) (**body length**) from the cast-on edge. *Optional: See "short-row shaping for the body" on page 29.*

 On the next round, knit ____ **back stitches**, place a second marker, knit to the end of the round (____ **front stitches**). You now have a marker at the beginning of the round and a second marker halfway around, marking the side "seams" of the sweater.

 On the next round, bind off or place on hold ____ **underarm stitches** at each side marker, with half of the underarm stitches coming before the marker and half after it. Remove the markers.

Set the body aside, placing its stitches on a spare needle or stitch holders.

③ Cast on and knit cuffs

 Using double-pointed needles and main color, cast on ____ **cuff stitches**. Join, being careful not to twist, place a marker at the beginning of the round, and knit in the round.   Work in your choice of ribbing until the cuff measures 2 inches (5 cm), or desired length.

④ Work sleeve increases

Change to stockinette stitch. Begin increasing for the sleeve as follows: On every 4th round, k1, increase 1, knit to just before last stitch, increase 1, k1.

When the stitches no longer fit on the double-pointed needles, change to the 16-inch (40-cm) circular needle.

Keep an eye on the shape of your sleeve and measure it against your model sweater or try your sleeve on after every few inches (cm) to make sure the sleeve is increasing at a comfortable rate. If your sleeve is becoming wide too quickly, start increasing every 6th round. If it is not widening quickly enough, start increasing every 3rd round.

 Continue increasing until you have ____ **sleeve stitches** and then work even until sleeve is ____ inches (cm) (**sleeve length**) from the cast-on edge.

 On the next round, bind off or place on hold ____ **underarm stitches** at the marker, with half of the underarm stitches coming before the marker and half after it. Remove the marker.

Set the sleeve aside, placing its stitches on a spare needle or stitch holders.

Make second sleeve the same way as the first, steps 3 and 4.

⑤ Join sleeves and body

Arrange the body and sleeve stitches on one long circular needle, as follows: Slip ____ **back yoke stitches** onto the needle, place a marker. Slip ____ left **sleeve yoke stitches** onto the needle, place a marker. Slip ____ **front yoke stitches** onto the needle, place a marker. Slip ____ right **sleeve yoke stitches** onto the needle, and place a marker in a different color to mark the beginning of the yoke

rounds. You should have ____ stitches (**total yoke stitches**).

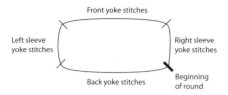

Front yoke stitches

Left sleeve yoke stitches

Right sleeve yoke stitches

Back yoke stitches

Beginning of round

6 Work yoke pattern bands

Work 2 rounds and increase or decrease to the nearest even multiple of your first pattern repeat, spacing the increases or decreases through the round(s).

With main color and contrasting color(s), follow the chart to set up the pattern, placing markers between the pattern repeats, if desired.

Work decreases as noted below, fudging between patterns and in each decrease round so that you end up with an even multiple of the next pattern repeat. See the information on pages 77–78 about placing the decrease rounds and the tips on page 14 about altering yoke depth.

Work the first pattern(s) until the yoke measures approximately ½ of the desired depth: ____ inches (cm) (.5 × ____ **yoke depth**).

First decrease round: On a plain round, (k2, k2tog) around.

Work the next pattern(s) until the yoke measures approximately ⅔ to ¾ of the desired depth: ____ inches (cm) (.66 to .75 × ____ **yoke depth**).

Second decrease round: On a plain round, (k1, k2tog) around.

Work the next pattern(s) until the yoke measures approximately 1 inch (2.5 cm) less than the desired depth: ____ inches (cm) (____ **yoke depth – 1 inch**).

Note: If you are going to work the optional short rows in step 7, work the pattern(s) until the yoke measures approximately 2 inches (5 cm) less than the desired depth: ____ inches (cm) (____ **yoke depth – 2 inches**).

Third decrease round: On a plain round, (k1, k2tog, k2tog) around.

7 Knit optional short rows and neckband

Optional: If desired, just after the last decrease round you can work short rows to raise the back neck. *See "short-row shaping at the back neck" on page 29.*

If necessary, work a round and adjust stitch count to ____ **neck stitches**.

Work neckband in your choice of ribbing for 1 inch (2.5 cm), or desired height of neckband. Bind off loosely in pattern.

8 Finish

Join each underarm opening with a seam, three-needle bind-off, or kitchener stitch, as desired.

Weave in the ends.

Cardigan with Horizontal Bands

This cardigan is decorated with just two charts. In the zigzag pattern at the cuffs, hem, and yoke, the body color is used for pattern and the accent is used for background. In the main part of the sweater, those relationships reverse, creating an interesting look that frames your sweater.

Each section of the yoke is knitted without decreases. Between charts, a few plain rounds are worked to allow you to decrease without interrupting the stitch patterns.

For a classic look, work with a background color plus one solid contrasting color. For a more fanciful design, work the contrasting stitches in a self-striping yarn or change colors every few rounds.

☑ Color patterns in bands on yoke and on lower body and sleeves

☑ Lower body and sleeves worked in the round to the armholes, then joined so the yoke can also be worked in the round

☑ Yoke decreases worked between pattern bands

☑ Front opening is steeked!

This illustration shows a sweater with a 40-inch (102-cm) body circumference and 24-inch (61-cm) body length in medium-weight singles (lopi-style) yarn with 4¾ stitches and 6¾ rows to the inch (19 stitches and 27 rows to 10 cm). Experiment with chunky or fine yarns—use a bit of extra ease with heavy yarns. Remember to use *your* gauge in planning your project.

Patterns: Zigzags and Stars (page 81) and the Alternating Geometric Pattern (page 80).

Get ready *yarn & needles*

Iceland
Cardigan *with* Horizontal Bands

Yarn

As long as the yarn is smooth and comes in the colors you want, it will work well in this design. Wool or a wool blend will make a warm winter garment; wool yarns are easiest to work with when steeking. A sweater made of cotton can be worn in other seasons or climates. If you choose a yarn that does not contain much wool, take extra care when securing and cutting the steeks—or work the body back and forth in one piece (as described on pages 164–166).

Any weight of yarn will work, but for the look of a traditional lopi-style sweater, I suggest a medium- or bulky-weight singles (unplied) yarn made of wool. If you make a lightweight cardigan, you will be able to fit more patterns and color changes into the yoke and the sweater will be more appropriate for wear by those who don't live in a snow belt, but the garment will take much longer to knit and the patterns will be less graphic because of their smaller dimensions.

Yarn guidelines, including a yardage estimate table, are on pages 20–22.

Knitting needles

In a size appropriate for the yarn you've chosen:

✦ Circular needle for body: for an adult sweater, use a needle at least 29 inches (74 cm) long

✦ Circular needle for sleeves and neckband: 16 inches (40 cm) long

✦ Double-pointed needles for cuffs: set of 4 or 5

Tip: Some knitters find that their gauge is more consistent if they knit the colorwork portions of a project on a needle that is one size larger than the needle they use for the solid areas. You may also prefer to use smaller needles (often two sizes smaller) when you work the ribbing on the body and the sleeve cuffs.

Needle guidelines, including tips on choosing lengths of circular needles and on working small tubes on circulars, are on pages 18–20.

Additional supplies

✦ Stitch markers
✦ Spare needle or stitch holders
✦ Large plastic pins
✦ Buttons (seven)
✦ Sewing needle and matching thread

Get set *stitches, gauge & size*	Iceland Cardigan *with* Horizontal Bands

Stitches and gauge

1 Select the pattern stitches for your sweater. Use the combination shown in the illustration on page 102 or choose your own combination of narrow pattern bands, either from this book or from a knitting-stitch library.

2 Make a gauge swatch in stockinette stitch.

Knit the swatch in the round to make sure you get an accurate gauge measurement. If you don't have a lot of experience with colorwork, make both a solid swatch and a colorwork swatch to see if you get the same gauge with the same size needle.

3 Measure your gauge. Write the stitch gauge and row gauge on the sweater-planning worksheet on page 107.

Size

1 Measure your favorite sweater or use the size charts on page 16 to determine the basic dimensions for your sweater. Write the measurements on the visual plan on page 106 and the sweater-planning worksheet on page 107.

2 Use the calculations on the worksheets on pages 107–109 to figure all the remaining numbers before you start, or just calculate each new number as you need it.

3 Transfer the resulting numbers to the visual plan on page 106 or the step-by-step instructions on pages 110–113, depending on how much guiding detail you would like to have while you knit.

Knit!   *option I: using a visual plan*

Iceland
Cardigan *with* Horizontal Bands

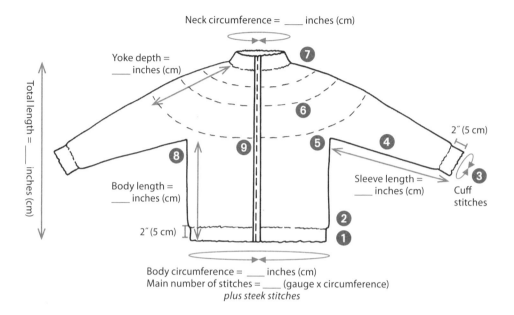

Neck circumference = ____ inches (cm)

Yoke depth = ____ inches (cm)

Total length = ____ inches (cm)

2″ (5 cm)

Body length = ____ inches (cm)

Sleeve length = ____ inches (cm)

Cuff stitches

2″ (5 cm)

Body circumference = ____ inches (cm)
Main number of stitches = ____ (gauge x circumference)
plus steek stitches

LOWER BODY

1 Cast on ____ stitches (90% of main number of stitches) plus ____ steek stitches and knit ribbing; note that steek stitches are worked in stockinette throughout and are not included in subsequent counts

2 Increase to ____ stitches (main number of stitches), change to stockinette stitch, and work to body length, knitting optional short rows if desired

SLEEVES

3 Cast on ____ cuff stitches and knit ribbing

4 Change to stockinette stitch and work sleeve; increase at even intervals along underarm to ____ sleeve stitches, then work even until sleeve reaches sleeve length

UPPER BODY

5 Join sleeves and body

6 Work yoke, decreasing between pattern bands as follows:

★ At ½ length, (k2, k2tog) around

★ At ⅔ to ¾ length, (k1, k2tog) around

★ At full length, (k1, k2tog, k2tog) around

FINISH

7 Work optional short rows and neckband and bind off

8 Open steek and work front bands

9 Join underarms and weave in ends

Knit! *option 2: using planning worksheets* Iceland Cardigan *with* Horizontal Bands

Measurements for project 6

	Calculation	Example	Description
Stitch gauge	___ stitches = 1 inch or 1 cm	**5** stitches = 1 inch	**Stitch gauge** is critical for knitting a sweater that fits properly.
Row gauge	___ rows = 1 inch or 1 cm	**6** rows = 1 inch	**Row gauge** is not critical for this sweater, because you measure the yoke as you go and work decreases at the designated measurements. It may help you determine whether a specific pattern will fit in the next area that you will work.
Body width	___ inches (cm)	**20** inches	Measure the **width** of the sweater body.
Body circumference	___ x 2 = ___ inches (cm)	20 x 2 = **40** inches	Double the body width for the **circumference of the sweater**.
Total length	___ inches (cm)	**24** inches	Measure the **length** of the sweater body from cast-on to shoulder.
Yoke depth	___ ÷ 4 = ___ inches (cm)	40 ÷ 4 = **10** inches	Measure the **yoke depth** or use the sweater proportions chart on page 14 to calculate the yoke depth. (See tips on page 14 for altering yoke depth.)
Body length	___ – ___ = ___ inches (cm)	24 – 10 = **14** inches	Subtract the yoke depth from the total body length to calculate the **length of the body from the cast-on edge to the armhole**.
Sleeve length	___ inches (cm)	**18** inches	Measure the **sleeve length** from the cuff edge to the underarm.
Upper sleeve circumference	___ x .40 = ___ inches (cm)	40 x .40 = **16** inches	Take 35 to 40 percent of the body circumference to calculate the **upper sleeve circumference**, depending on whether you want tighter (.35) or looser (.40) sleeves.
Neck circumference	___ inches (cm)	**16** inches	Measure the **circumference around the neck** or use the sweater proportions chart on page 14 to calculate the neck circumference.

A — Yoke depth
B — Body length
C — Sleeve length

Stitch counts for project 6

		Calculation	Example	Description
a	Main number of stitches	___ x ___ = ___ stitches	40 x 5 = **200** stitches	Multiply the body circumference by your stitch gauge to calculate the **main number of stitches**. Round this up or down as necessary to equal an even multiple of the pattern stitches you've chosen. (You can adjust your stitch count slightly between pattern bands.)
b	Stitches to cast on	___ x .9 = ___ stitches	200 x .9 = **180** stitches 180 stitches is a multiple of 4	Take 90 percent of the main number of stitches to calculate the **number of stitches to cast on**. Round up or down to the nearest multiple of your chosen ribbing.
c	Steek stitches (sweater front opening)	7 stitches	3, 5, or 7 stitches	You will work 3, 5, or 7 stitches at the front of the sweater for the **steek at the sweater front opening**.

👉 **VERY IMPORTANT NOTE:** The steek stitches are not included in any of the stitch counts that follow. They are worked—bottom to top, with no increases, decreases, or other alterations—following one of the charts on page 163, and are not in the body patterns.

		Calculation	Example	Description
d	Back stitches	___ ÷ 2 = ___ stitches	200 ÷ 2 = **100** stitches	Divide the main number of stitches in half to determine the **number of stitches in the back.**
e	Front section stitches	___ ÷ 2 = ___ stitches	100 ÷ 2 = **50** stitches	Divide the number of back stitches in half to determine the **number of stitches in each front section.**
f	Sleeve stitches	___ x ___ = ___ stitches	16 x 5 = **80** stitches	Multiply the upper sleeve circumference by your stitch gauge to calculate the **number of sleeve stitches** required at the top of the sleeve.
g	Underarm stitches	___ x 2 = ___ stitches	5 x 2 = **10** stitches	Multiply your stitch gauge by 2 to calculate how many stitches to set aside for a 2-inch (5-cm) **underarm seam.** (Metric: Divide the number of stitches in 10 cm by 2 to reach the same number.)
h	Back yoke stitches	___ – ___ = ___ stitches	100 – 10 = **90** stitches	Subtract the number of underarm stitches from the back stitches to calculate how many **stitches from the back** will remain for the **yoke**.

Stitch counts for project 6 (continued)

		Calculation	Example	Description
i	Front yoke section stitches	___ – ___ = ___ stitches	50 – 5 = **45** stitches	Subtract half the number of underarm stitches from the front section stitches to calculate how many **stitches from each front section** will remain for the **yoke**. *Note:* The front yoke area will also contain the extra steek stitches.
j	Sleeve yoke stitches	___ – ___ = ___ stitches	80 – 10 = **70** stitches	Subtract the number of underarm stitches from the sleeve stitches to calculate how many **stitches from each sleeve** will remain for the **yoke**.
k	Total yoke stitches	___ + ___ + ___ + ___ + ___ = ___ stitches	45 + 45 + 90 + 70 + 70 = **320** stitches	To determine the **total number of stitches at the beginning of the yoke**, add both sets of front yoke stitches, the back yoke stitches, the left sleeve yoke stitches, and the right sleeve yoke stitches. *Note:* The steek stitches are still worked but are not included in this count.
l	Neck stitches	___ x ___ = ___ stitches	16 x 5 = **80** stitches **80** stitches is a multiple of 2 and of 4	Multiply the neck circumference by the stitch gauge to calculate the **neck stitches**, which represent the number of stitches that remain after the yoke decreasing. Round this up or down to a multiple of your chosen ribbing pattern.
m	Cuff stitches	___ stitches	**40** stitches 40 stitches is a multiple of 4	After you knit the body of your sweater, wrap the ribbing around your wrist and count the **number of stitches for the cuff**. For a rough estimate of this number, divide the main number of stitches by 5. Round up or down to a multiple of 4 for working k2, p2 ribbing.

Need a slightly different stitch count? Increase or decrease by a few.

This example has been set up with numbers that happen to result in an adult's sweater with a finished chest measurement of 40″ (102 cm) that falls to just below the waistline. If you're not that size, and only a few of us will be, use the guidelines on pages 14–17 and measurements you gather for yourself to make a sweater that is customized for its wearer.

Knit! *option 3: a step-by-step project sheet* Iceland Cardigan *with* Horizontal Bands

Use this project sheet if you are not yet comfortable working directly from the sweater-planning diagram. With time, you'll find that you no longer need to refer to these instructions.

Do the calculations on the planning worksheets on pages 107–109 so you have the numbers to fill in here.

This worksheet is written to reflect the color changes and pattern sequences in the sample sweater. Read through to understand the process, then adjust to suit the color changes and pattern sequences that *you* choose.

1 Cast on and knit ribbing

With a 29-inch (74-cm) circular needle and the contrasting color, cast on ____ stitches (____ **stitches to cast on *plus* ____ steek stitches**). Join, being careful not to twist. The beginning of the round is the center stitch of the steek stitches. Place a marker on each side of the steek, and knit in the round.

 VERY IMPORTANT: Remember that the steek stitches are ***not*** included in the stitch counts! The number of steek stitches at the center front will remain constant, and all shaping will be done in the main body of the sweater.

Work in your choice of ribbing, with the steek stitches in stockinette, until the

ribbing measures 2 inches (5 cm), or desired length.

2 Work lower body and optional short rows

Change to stockinette stitch (knit every round), and increase to ____ stitches (**main number of stitches**) on the first round as follows: Work the steek stitches at the beginning of the round, then *k9, increase 1, repeat from * to the remaining steek stitches, and work the steek stitches at the end of the round. Fudge if necessary to make sure you have a number of stitches that works with your pattern repeat.

As you begin working the patterns, work the steek stitches following one of the charts on page 163, using the same colors as the body. If you are using different colors in your contrasting sections, change colors at the center stitch of the steek. When you work solid portions of the body, work the steek stitches in the same color as the body.

On the next round, work the first few steek stitches, then knit ____ **front section stitches**, place a side marker, knit ____ **back stitches**, place a second side marker, knit to the end of the round (____**front section stitches** and remaining steek stitches). You now have four markers: two surrounding the steek stitches and two at the side "seams" of the sweater.

B Continuing with the contrasting color and adding the main color, work the pattern of your choice. Then, using the main color only, work even in stockinette stitch until body measures ____ inches (cm) (**body length**) from the cast-on edge.

Optional: See "short-row shaping for the body" on page 29.

g On the next round, bind off or place on hold ____ **underarm stitches** at each side marker, with half of the underarm stitches coming before the marker and half after it. Remove the markers.

Set the body aside, placing its stitches on a spare needle or stitch holders.

③ Cast on and knit cuffs

m Using double-pointed needles and contrasting color, cast on ____ **cuff stitches**. Join, being careful not to twist, place a marker at the beginning of the round, and knit in the round.

Work in your choice of ribbing until the cuff measures 2 inches (5 cm), or desired length.

④ Work sleeve increases

Change to stockinette stitch. On the first round, increase to an even multiple of the pattern stitch you have chosen, spacing the increases evenly within the round.

Add the main color and begin working the pattern of your choice. **AT THE SAME TIME,** begin increasing for the

sleeve as follows: On every 4th round, k1, increase 1, knit to just before last stitch, increase 1, k1. As you work the increases, incorporate the new stitches into the established pattern.

After completing the colorwork pattern, with main color only, continue working in stockinette stitch and increasing as established on either side of the marker. When the stitches no longer fit comfortably on the double-pointed needles, change to the 16-inch (40-cm) circular needle.

Keep an eye on the shape of your sleeve and measure it against your model sweater or try your sleeve on after every few inches (cm) to make sure the sleeve is increasing at a comfortable rate. If your sleeve is becoming wide too quickly, start increasing every 6th round. If it is not widening quickly enough, start increasing every 3rd round.

f

c

Continue increasing until you have ____ **sleeve stitches** and then work even until sleeve is ____ inches (cm) (**sleeve length**) from the cast-on edge.

g

On the next round, bind off or place on hold ____ **underarm stitches** at the marker, with half of the underarm stitches coming before the marker and half after it. Remove the marker.

Set the sleeve aside, placing its stitches on a spare needle or stitch holders.

Make the second sleeve the same way as the first, steps 3 and 4.

⑤ Join sleeves and body

Arrange the body and sleeve stitches on one long circular needle, as follows: Slip first half of the **steek stitches** (and the first marker) onto the needle, then follow with ____ **right front yoke section stitches**, place a marker, ____ right **sleeve yoke stitches**, place a marker, ____ **back yoke stitches**, place a marker, ____ left **sleeve yoke stitches**, place a marker, ____ **left front yoke section stitches**, and the second half of the **steek stitches** (with its marker). You should have ____ stitches (____ **total yoke stitches** *plus* ____ **steek stitches**).

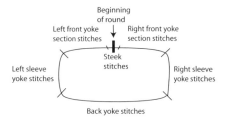

Beginning of round

Left front yoke section stitches — Right front yoke section stitches

Steek stitches

Left sleeve yoke stitches — Right sleeve yoke stitches

Back yoke stitches

⑥ Work yoke pattern

Work 2 rounds and increase or decrease to the nearest even multiple of your first pattern repeat, spacing the increases or decreases through the round(s).

With main color and contrasting color(s), follow the chart to set up the first pattern, placing markers between the pattern repeats, if desired.

Work decreases as noted below, fudging between patterns and in each decrease round so that you end up with an even multiple of the next pattern repeat. See the information on pages 77–78 about

placing the decrease rounds and the tips on page 14 about altering yoke depth.

Work the pattern(s) until the yoke measures approximately ½ of the desired depth: ____ inches (cm) (.5 × ____ **yoke depth**).

First decrease round: On a plain round, (k2, k2tog) around.

Work the next pattern(s) until the yoke measures approximately ⅔ to ¾ of the desired depth: ____ inches (cm) (.66 to .75 × ____ **yoke depth**).

Second decrease round: On a plain round, (k1, k2tog) around.

Work the next pattern(s) until the yoke measures approximately 1 inch (2.5 cm) less than the desired depth: ____ inches (cm) (____ **yoke depth – 1 inch**).

Note: If you are going to work the optional short rows in step 7, work the pattern(s) until the yoke measures approximately 2 inches (5 cm) less than the desired depth: ____ inches (cm) (____ **yoke depth – 2 inches**).

Third decrease round: On a plain round, (k1, k2tog, k2tog) around.

⑦ Knit optional short rows and neckband

Optional: If desired, just after the last decrease round you can work more short rows to raise the back neck. *See "short-row shaping at the back neck" on page 29.*

If necessary, work a round and adjust stitch count to ____ **neck stitches**.

Work neckband in your choice of ribbing for 1 inch (2.5 cm), or desired height of neckband. Bind off loosely in pattern.

8 Knit front bands

Secure the front steek and cut it open (see page 164).

Button band: With right side facing, using main color and the long circular needle, pick up and knit stitches along the right front (for men) or the left front (for women).

Tip: When I do this, I look at the gauge of the sweater. If the sweater is at 5 stitches and 7 rows to 1 inch (2.5 cm), I pick up 5 stitches for every 7 rows of knitting (pick up 3, skip 1, pick up 2, skip 1, and repeat). I do work my ribbing on a smaller needle than I have used for the body of the sweater, so it doesn't flare out.

Work the button band in your choice of ribbing for 1 inch (2.5 cm), or to the desired width.

Optional: If desired, you can work a turning ridge (one row of purl stitches worked with the right side toward you) and a facing for the button band. The facing will have as many rows as the band and will be turned to the inside and stitched in place. A facing is not necessary but has the advantage of covering the cut edge of the steek.

Bind off loosely in pattern.

With the large plastic pins, mark the placement for the buttons. Place one button near the top of the band and one near the bottom, and space the remaining buttons evenly in between.

Buttonhole band: On the left front (for men) or the right front (for women), work as for button band until just under ½ inch (1.25 cm) has been completed, ending with a wrong-side row. On the next row (right side), work buttonholes (see pages 169–170) to correspond to the locations of the pins on the button band.

Continue as you did for the button band. If you worked a facing on the band, work buttonholes on the facing as well, placing them just under ½ inch (1.25 cm) from the completion of the facing.

9 Finish

Join each underarm opening with a seam, three-needle bind-off, or kitchener stitch, as desired.

If you have worked facings, stitch their long edges in place to cover the cut edges of the steek. On the buttonhole band, stitch the matching buttonholes together loosely around their edges.

Weave in the ends.

Sew on the buttons.

Ireland

When I was in junior high school, my grandmother made me an elaborately patterned sweater out of electric-blue yarn. She took me to the yarn store and let me pick out yarn, and then showed me a book of pattern stitches and let me choose my favorites. I chose honeycomb cables, diamonds, and bobbles. I kept this sweater until a few years ago although, not surprisingly, it hadn't fit me in quite some time. Finally, because I knew my grandmother would rather have me give away a garment she had made than keep it folded up in a closet unused, I gave it to a friend with a teenage daughter.

During the 1970s and '80s, my grandmother must have made at least two dozen sweaters decorated with the cable designs she called "Irish patterns." Today sweaters knitted with these elaborate cable patterns are known as Aran sweaters, named after the islands with which they are identified. The three islands of Aran, located off of the west coast of Ireland, are called Inishmore (*Inis Mór*, Big Island), Inishmaan (*Inis Meáin*, Middle Island), and Inisheer (*Inis Oírr*, East Island). With a stark, damp, and windy environment, it is no surprise that heavy woolen sweaters are made here.

Developed in the first half of the twentieth century, Aran sweaters were inspired by fishermen's ganseys, which were knitted in the round and decorated with panels of knit and purl stitches and simple cables. Men wore the sweaters along with several layers of woven shirts, vests, and jackets. The usual design had a plain lower body with a patterned yoke. Sometime between 1920 and 1936, local knitters began embellishing the entire body and sleeves with dense cable patterns, and making garments not for work but for dressy wear.

Early Arans were knitted entirely or partly in the round, using the techniques taken from gansey knitting.

But over time, as the sweaters were adapted for commercial markets, they began to be knitted flat to make it easier to write standard patterns and to make it simpler for contract knitters to knit the sweaters in standard sizes. This is also when the heavy, natural yarn that is associated with Aran sweaters today first came into common use. The thick, cream-colored yarn is called *baineen* (pronounced *bawneen*), which means natural. The light color of this yarn shows off the patterns better than dark colors, and the heavier weight yarn works up much faster than fine gansey yarn.

During the 1960s and '70s, raglan shaping was popular, but designs featuring the traditional saddle shoulder became fashionable again in the 1990s. Today, most Arans are knitted flat in pieces, then sewn together. This is the technique I prefer, not because I can't figure out how many stitches I need with patterns that draw in as much as cabling does but because I like working back across the wrong-side rows, "knitting the knits and purling the purls" without thinking about the cable pattern. I find that when these rest rows are worked from the right side, as they are in circular knitting, it is not as easy to keep track of my pattern or to count the rows between cable crossings. I've included information on pages 160–161 for those who want to knit their Aran sweaters in the round.

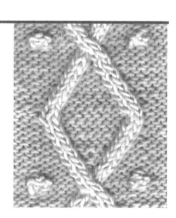

CHAPTER 5 HIGHLIGHTS

Skills
- ☑ Knitting cables
- ☑ Reading cable charts

Techniques
- ☑ Bobbles
- ☑ Preventing cable flare

Garment styling
- ☑ Saddle-shoulder construction
- ☑ Worked flat in pieces, with in-the-round adaptation optional

Techniques

The only unusual technique required for Aran knitting is cable making. Although cables look quite complicated, they are actually easy to make. You just slip some stitches to a spare cable needle, and knit them out of order. Holding the cable needle to the front or back of the work while you knit a few other stitches allows you to create cables that lean toward the left and the right. Hold the cable needle to the front for left-crossing cables and to the back for right-crossing cables.

Left-crossing cable

To make a left-crossing cable, you hold the cable needle in front of the work. For a four-stitch, 2-over-2 cable:

1. Slip 2 stitches to a cable needle.

2. Hold the cable needle in front of the work.

3. Knit the next 2 stitches from the left needle.

4. Knit the 2 stitches from the cable needle.

Right-crossing cable

To make a right-crossing cable, you hold the cable needle in back of the work. For a four-stitch, 2-over-2 cable:

1. Slip 2 stitches to a cable needle.

2. Hold the cable needle in back of the work.

3. Knit the next 2 stitches from the left needle.

4. Knit the 2 stitches from the cable needle.

Counting rows between cable crossings

Counting the rows between cable crossings is much easier when you are looking at the back (wrong side) of your knitting.

Above the cable crossing, which will look twisted (1), locate the first row of purl bumps that runs straight across the entire cable (2). It may be slightly distorted but you will see a distinct bump for each stitch. Pay attention only to the purl bumps that look like this: ⌒. Count that row and all of the rows above it.

Making bobbles

Bobbles are little knitted buttons or knobs that add texture to the surface of knitting. Bobbles can be made larger or smaller by changing the number of stitches or rows worked.

A bobble is usually indicated by a large, filled-in circle on a chart. At the bobble indicator, you can work a bobble of any size that you like. If you prefer to work the chart without the bobbles, work the stitch as a plain knit or purl to match the surrounding stitches.

To make a small bobble

1. Work up to the stitch where you want to make the bobble. (K1f, k1b, k1f) all in that next stitch.

2. Turn and p3, turn, k3, turn, p3, turn.

3. Slip 1, k2tog, psso (1 stitch remains). Continue working the rest of the row as charted.

To make a large bobble

1. Work up to the stitch where you want to make the bobble. (K1f, k1b, k1f, k1b, k1f) all in that next stitch.

2. Turn and p5, turn, k5, turn, p5, turn.

3. Slip 2, k3tog, p2sso (1 stitch remains). Continue working the rest of the row as charted.

Chart symbols used in cable patterns

Many different systems of cable symbols are used by different publishers. Unfortunately, there is no one standard, and this can be a reason that some people think cables are difficult!

I've chosen these symbols you see in this book because I think they are easy to follow and they create a chart that looks like the knitted cable. The Aran sweaters in this book are designed to be knitted back and forth in pieces, but I've included a legend for interpreting the charts for circular knitting as well.

These chart symbols for cables provide hints as to what you need to do. The cable will lean in the same direction as the diagonal line in the middle of the cable symbol.

To knit a cable directly from the symbol without looking up the definition:

1. *Transfer the stitches on the right part of the cable symbol to the cable needle.* Start by looking at the right half of the cable symbol.

   Count the number of stitches on the right part of the cable symbol. This is the number of stitches to put on the cable needle.

   If the lines representing the stitches on the right part of the cable symbol look like they *cross in front* of the other stitches (forming a diagonal line up and to the left), hold the cable needle to the *front* of your work.

   If the lines representing the stitches on the right part of the cable symbol look like they *cross in back* of the other stitches (the left set of stitches forms a diagonal line up and to the right), hold the cable needle to the *back* of your work.

Left-crossing cable Right-crossing cable

2 stitches 2 stitches

2 stitches cross in front

2 stitches cross in back

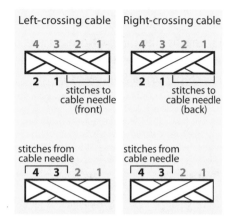

2. *Knit (or sometimes purl) the stitches on the left part of the cable symbol.*

3. *Knit (or sometimes purl) the stitches held on the cable needle.*

That's it!

Here's the same step-by-step process for the 3-stitch cable crossings that involve knit stitches crossing over a purl stitch:

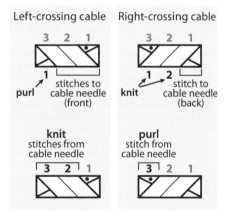

1. *Same as for 4-stitch cable crossings.*

2. *Knit or purl the stitches on the left part of the cable symbol.*

3. *Knit or purl the stitches held on the cable needle.*

Becoming comfortable with cables

As you knit, learn to look at your knitting and figure out where the cable stitches should move next. In most cases you are moving one set of knit stitches in front of another set of knit or purl stitches to draw a shape, such as a diamond or a rope. Try to think about what cable shape you are drawing as you move the stitches, and use the knitting you've completed as a guide.

You'll find that often you won't need to refer to the charts after you complete one or two repeats. In fact, you may eventually find that it's easier to knit cables by copying a photo or a swatch than by working from a chart or line-by-line instructions, just as many Irish knitters memorized cable patterns from the backs of their friends' sweaters during Sunday morning church services!

Symbols used in cable charts

Cable symbols vary widely from one charting system to another. Don't worry about memorizing this. If it helps you, great. If not, just file it away for future reference.

In the abbreviation section of this chart, C means a cable made of all knit stitches and T indicates a cable made with knit stitches crossing in front of purl stitches.

Symbol	Translation	Abbreviation
	Knit (as seen from right side of fabric)	K
	Purl (as seen from right side of fabric)	P
	Bobble: Work bobble as described in pattern	
	Slip 1 stitch to cable needle and hold in front, k1, k1 from cable needle	C2L (2-stitch cable, left-crossing)
	Slip 1 stitch to cable needle and hold in back, k1, k1 from cable needle	C2R (2-stitch cable, right-crossing)
	Slip 2 stitches to cable needle and hold in front, k2, k2 from cable needle	C4L (4-stitch cable, left-crossing)
	Slip 2 stitches to cable needle and hold in back, k2, k2 from cable needle	C4R (4-stitch cable, right-crossing)
	Slip 3 stitches to cable needle and hold in front, k3, k3 from cable needle	C6L (6-stitch cable, left-crossing)
	Slip 3 stitches to cable needle and hold in back, k3, k3 from cable needle	C6R (6-stitch cable, right-crossing)
	Slip 3 stitches to cable needle and hold in front, k2, k3 from cable needle	C5L (5-stitch cable, left-crossing)
	Slip 2 stitches to cable needle and hold in back, k3, k2 from cable needle	C5R (5-stitch cable, right-crossing)
	Slip 2 stitches to cable needle and hold in front, p1, k2 from cable needle	T3L (3-stitch k/p cable, left-crossing)
	Slip 1 stitch to cable needle and hold in back, k2, p1 from cable needle	T3R (3-stitch k/p cable, right-crossing)

Special notes about Aran-style sweater design

Aran sweaters are perhaps the most complex to design of all sweater types. I've included a lot of extra help in this section to get you started. But just as with the other types of sweaters, after you design a couple of Arans, you'll find that you don't need anything except the schematic drawings to plan and knit your custom design.

The body of an Aran-style sweater features a center panel that is flanked on either side by other cable patterns. To balance the design, it is traditional to reverse the direction of cable crossings in the patterns on either side of the center panel. For example, a diamond stitch (as shown in the drawing below, with bobbles) may be

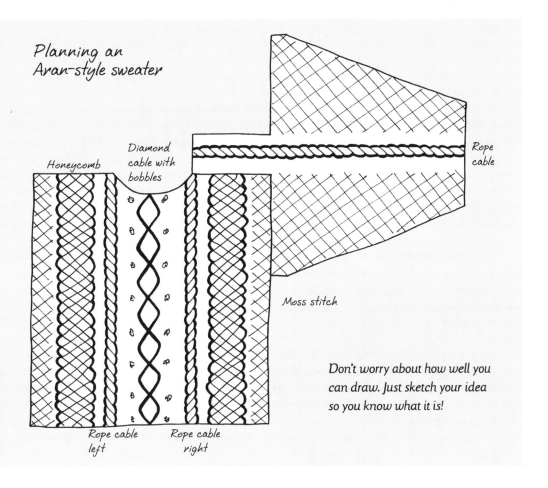

Planning an Aran-style sweater

Honeycomb

Diamond cable with bobbles

Rope cable

Moss stitch

Rope cable left

Rope cable right

Don't worry about how well you can draw. Just sketch your idea so you know what it is!

the center panel with left-crossing rope cables on one side and right-crossing rope cables on the other. On the sweater concept sketched here, there is also a panel of honeycomb outside the rope cables.

Sometimes a column of one or two (or more) plain knit or purl stitches is added between panels.

The sleeves also have a center panel that runs along the outside of the arm, with mirrored cables on either side. The center panel on the sleeves may be the same as the center panel on the sweater body (or a smaller version of that pattern), or it may be one of the cables that is used on the sides of the body. The center panel on the sleeve has to be narrow enough to fit on the saddle shoulder, which should not exceed 4 inches (10 cm) for adults or 2 inches (5 cm) for children.

On the outside edges of both the body and sleeves, a simple texture stitch, such as moss stitch (page 128), is used. This makes it easier to work the increases on the sleeves and later to sew the pieces together.

When you plan your design, remember that it is easier if the vertical repeats of your cable crossings either match or work together with a nice rhythm. Look not only at the individual pattern repeats but at how the patterns coordinate with each other. You can make the cable sequences as complicated as you like after you're familiar with cabling.

Cables and gauges and stitch counts

Even when worked with the same yarn and needles, you'll find that cable patterns vary from each other in both stitch and row gauge more than other types of pattern stitches.

Some cable patterns are loose and open, with a lot of plain stitches that usually form a reverse stockinette stitch background. Examples are the diamonds (pages 130–131). Others are dense and thick, with a lot of crossed stitches that draw the fabric in, the way ribbing does. Examples of these are the honeycomb patterns (page 129).

When you use open and airy cables, you can treat them the same as you would any knit-and-purl texture stitch and work your ribbing on the normal 90 to 100 percent of the number of stitches in the main body of the sweater.

When you use dense cables in the body of a sweater, you will need to increase before you begin the cable pattern to make sure the cable areas don't draw in more than your ribbing and produce a funny bulge in your sweater. See the swatches on the following pages for an example of this. You can increase a stitch or two for each cable crossing, or begin your ribbing with about 80 percent (.8) of the main number of stitches.

When you bind off for the neck and shoulders of a sweater, you may find that you like the results better if you decrease once in the middle of each cable repeat to prevent the edges of the fabric from flaring out. This is particularly important if you are binding off several rows away from a cable crossing.

Be careful when you measure pieces knitted with cables. Just like ribbing, you can either leave the piece relaxed or stretch it slightly. When you measure, treat your knitted pieces the same way you treated your swatches to make sure you obtain the results you want.

Swatches provide lots of useful information!

Knitting a cable swatch

To get a good swatch of a cable pattern, you need to add a border of extra rows and stitches to your swatch. These extra stitches give you room to pin out the swatch so you can accurately measure the cable panel. I like garter stitch, because it helps the swatch lie flat. If you plan to include any plain stitches between the cables in your sweater, add them onto your swatch as well.

Always wash your cable swatches before you measure them. In some yarns, cables open up quite a bit when washed. If you make your sweater calculations using unwashed swatches, you may find that your sweater becomes several inches too wide when you wash it. It may also grow in length.

Don't forget to record the needle size you used. I do this by tying knots in the tail of yarn from the cast-on. I tie 4 knots for a size-4 needle, 6 knots for a size 6, and so forth.

A basic swatch of a cable pattern

At the bottom of this page is an example of a swatch for a honeycomb pattern that is 24 stitches wide (three repeats of an 8-stitch motif; this is the pattern at the bottom of page 129). We're also going to put a 4-stitch border of garter stitch on each side.

1. Cast on 32 stitches (4 garter stitch + 24 cable + 4 garter stitch).

2. Knit 6 rows (garter stitch) for an edging.

3. Set up the cable pattern as follows: K4 (garter-stitch edge), work 24 stitches of honeycomb chart, k4 (garter-stitch edge).

4. Continue to work the patterns as established until the swatch is about 4 inches (10 cm) high or you have completed between 1 and 3 pattern repeats.

5. Knit 6 rows and bind off.

Basic cable swatch

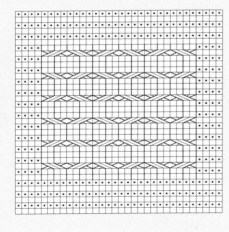

A swatch for the same pattern, with adjusted stitch counts
The example at the bottom of this page shows how to increase stitches above an edging, like garter stitch or ribbing, to accommodate the tendency of cables to draw in.

Both of these swatches have three full repeats of the
8-stitch honeycomb pattern (page 129) and a garter-
stitch border of 6 rows (top and bottom) and 4 stitches
(right and left edges). The swatches have been knitted
at the same gauge. In both cases, the light gray shading
shows one repeat of the cable pattern being sampled.

*Large versions of
both charts are on
pages 126 and 127.*

The only difference is cable flare.

For the swatch on page 124, 32 stitches were cast on
and the swatch was knitted on that number from start to
finish.

For the swatch on this page, 26 stitches were cast on.
In row 7, 6 increases were placed, one at the base of each
future cable crossing (total 32 stitches). At the end of the
swatch, in the first row of the garter-stitch border, those
6 stitches were decreased out again, one for each cable
crossing (back to 26 stitches). The dark gray sections of
the chart are "no stitch" space holders for the stitches
that are added (in row 7) or decreased out (in row 31).

Swatch with adjusted stitch counts

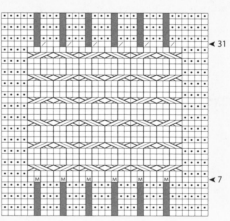

Swatching for smooth cable transitions

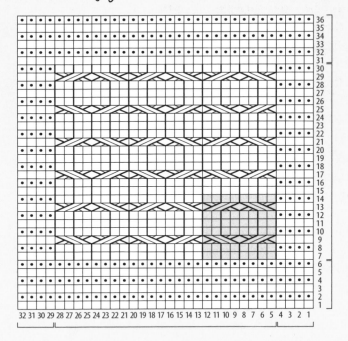

Chart for plain swatch

Notes for both charts

➤ The light gray shading shows the repeat of the cable stitch being sampled; each dark gray area on the adjusted chart is a placeholder (no stitch).

Stitches:

➤ Stitches 1–4 and 29–32 are the garter-stitch border.

➤ Stitches 5–28 include three horizontal repeats of the pattern stitch.

Rows:

➤ Rows 1–6 and 31–36 are the garter-stitch border.

➤ Rows 7–30 include three vertical repeats of the pattern stitch.

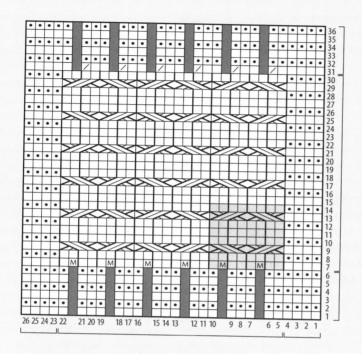

Chart for swatch with adjusted stitch counts below and above cables

Remember that Aran-style sweaters

✿ Use more yarn than less heavily textured designs

✿ Have more stitches to the inch (because the cables pull the stitches together horizontally)

✿ Have more rows to the inch (because the cables pull the stitches together vertically, too)

M	make1
/	k2tog
■	no stitch

Pattern stitches

Moss stitch

Worked over an even number of stitches.

Repeat:
2 stitches by 4 rows

Rope cables

Rope cables can be worked over any number of stitches. They are made of groups of knit stitches that cross over each other. The most common are 4- and 6-stitch rope cables. The cables can cross either to the left or to the right.

4-stitch rope cables

Left-crossing   Right-crossing

Repeat for each: 8 stitches by 6 rows

6-stitch rope cables

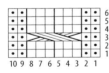

Left-crossing   Right-crossing

Repeat for each: 10 stitches by 6 rows

4-stitch left-crossing cable   4-stitch right-crossing cable

6-stitch left-crossing cable   6-stitch right-crossing cable

Honeycomb

Honeycomb can be worked with 2- or 4-stitch cable crossings. The patterns are known as 4-stitch and 8-stitch honeycomb because of the total number of stitches required in a repeat to accommodate the paired cable crossings. The 4-stitch version consists of pairs of 2-stitch crossings (1 over 1). The 8-stitch version consists of pairs of 4-stitch crossings (2 over 2).

Honeycomb cables have no purls within their pattern repeat. If you would like, you can add 2 plain purl stitches on either side of a honeycomb panel to separate it from adjacent cables.

The light-colored boxes on the photographs correspond to the charts.

4-stitch honeycomb

Repeat:

4 stitches by 4 rows

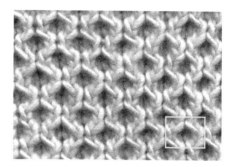

8-stitch honeycomb

Repeat:

8 stitches by 8 rows

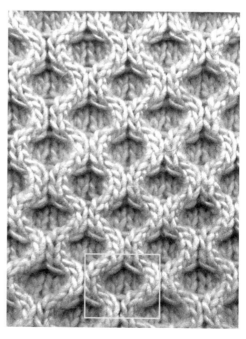

Diamond panels

Diamonds can also have left- or right-slanting cable crossings. The only difference between the two panels on this page is the direction of the cable crossing on row 1. The diamond outline is knitted in stockinette stitch (knit stitches) on a background of reverse stockinette (purl stitches). The knit stitches cross over purl stitches to form the outline of the diamond.

Diamond with bobbles,
with left-crossing cable

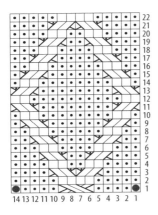

Repeat:

14 stitches

by 22 rows

Diamond with bobbles,
with right-crossing cable

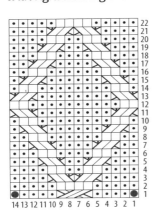

Repeat:

14 stitches

by 22 rows

If you don't like bobbles, work a regular purl
stitch in place of each bobble on the charts.

These diamonds have moss stitch instead of plain purls inside the diamond shape. To center the moss stitch in the diamond, I worked this cable over an odd number of stitches. I did not include bobbles on these charts, but you can easily add them.

The light-colored boxes on the photographs correspond to the charts.

Diamond with moss-stitch center, with left-crossing cable

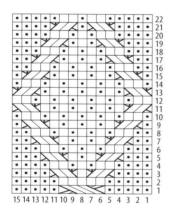

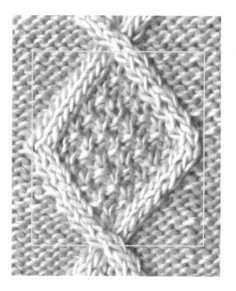

Repeat:

15 stitches

by 22 rows

Diamond with moss-stitch center, with right-crossing cable

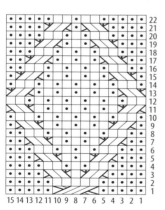

Repeat:

15 stitches

by 22 rows

131

Poncho

This poncho is made of two rectangles that are sewn to-gether after the knitting is complete. You can make both rectangles with the same cable panels or make one cabled piece and one plain piece. The poncho is easy to design because there is no shaping, and it will give you plenty of practice measuring cable gauge, planning a design, and knitting cables.

When you plan your design, remember that it is easier if the vertical repeats of your cable crossings match or follow a simple-to-remember rhythm.

✔ *Measuring and working with cable gauges*
✔ *Planning a design with cable panels*
✔ *Knitting cables*

The example shows a poncho made from two pieces about 21 inches (53 cm) wide by about 37 inches (94 cm) long, worked in chunky-weight yarn with a stockinette gauge of 3 stitches and 4½ rows to the inch (12 stitches and 18 rows to 10 cm). Because cable patterns draw in, the cable gauge is about 3½ stitches and 5 rows to the inch (14 stitches and 20 rows to 10 cm).

Patterns: Moss Stitch (page 128), 4-stitch Honeycomb (page 129, and 6-stitch Rope Cables (page 128).

Get ready   *yarn & needle*

Yarn

Smooth yarn will show off texture patterns best. Choose a tightly spun yarn for a wind-resistant poncho with excellent cable definition, and a loosely spun yarn for a softer poncho with more relaxed cables.

Any weight of yarn will work, but for practice I suggest a chunky-weight yarn and U.S. size 9 or 10 (5.5 or 6 mm) knitting needles.

Yarn quantities vary, depending on size. You'll need roughly the same amount as for a sweater.

Yarn guidelines, including a yardage estimate table for sweaters, are on pages 20–22.

Knitting needle

In a size appropriate for the yarn you've chosen:

✦ Straight or circular needle(s)

Needle guidelines are on pages 18–20.

Additional supplies
✦ Stitch markers

Get set   *stitches, gauge & size*

Stitches and gauge

1   Select the cable panels and side stitch for your poncho. Use the patterns shown on the sample illustration, or choose your combination of stitches either from this book or from a knitting-stitch library.

When you select cables, remember that the poncho will have one main center panel, surrounded by other cables that are mirror images on each side of the center.

2   Sketch the arrangement of your cable panels on the poncho planning diagram at the bottom of page 136.

Make gauge swatches of:

☆   Moss stitch, or the side stitch of your choice, and

☆   Each cable panel. If you are using any small patterns, you may decide to swatch these on either side of a larger cable panel, instead of making separate swatches.

Place the cable swatches on a flat surface to see how you like the arrangement of stitches. Rework your cable-planning sketch if necessary.

3 Measure your stitch gauge for the side stitch and write it on the planning worksheet on page 137.

Measure the width of each cable swatch and estimate how many panels you will need for the desired width; make sure you don't measure the garter-stitch border on each side of your swatch.

Record the cable-width measurements on the planning worksheet on page 137.

Check to see that these add up to the correct measurement for the poncho width.

4 *Optional:* Make a swatch of the combined cable panels and side stitch for half of the poncho and the center panel.

You don't need to do this step, although I never skip it because it helps me see what the entire piece will look like and practice knitting the combination of cables. I sometimes change my mind about whether or not I want plain stitches between my cable panels when I knit this swatch.

Size

1 Determine how wide and long you want your poncho to be and write the measurements in the boxes on the planning worksheet on page 137.

★ Child: Each piece approximately 14 inches (35.5 cm) wide by 25 inches (63.5 cm) long

★ Adult: Each piece approximately 21 inches (53 cm) wide by 37 inches (94 cm) long

2 Use the calculations on the worksheet to figure all the remaining numbers before you start, or just calculate each new number as you need it.

3 Transfer the numbers to the visual plan on page 136 or the step-by-step instructions on page 139, depending on how much guiding detail you would like to have while you knit.

Knit! *option I: using a visual plan*

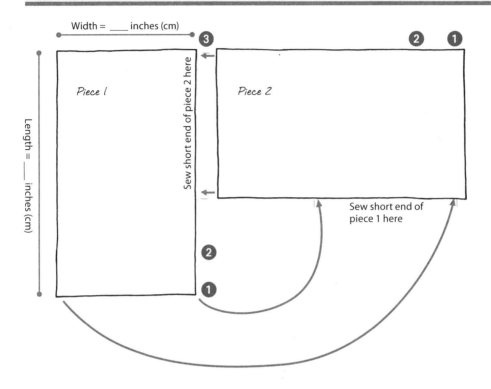

1. Cast on ____ stitches
2. Work cable patterns
3. Bind off

Repeat steps 1 to 3 for the second piece, using the same or different patterns.

4. Sew the two pieces together as shown

Poncho planning diagram

Sketch your cable arrangements

Knit! *option 2: using a planning worksheet*   Ireland Poncho

Poncho measurements

	Calculation	Example	Description
Width	____ inches (cm)	**21** inches	Measure the desired **width** of each poncho piece.
Length	____ inches (cm)	**37** inches	Measure the desired **length** of each poncho piece.

Gauge measurements for project 7

	Calculation	Example	Description
Stitch gauge for side stitch	____ stitches = 1 inch or 1 cm	**5** stitches = 1 inch	**Stitch gauge** is critical for knitting a poncho that comes out the desired size.
Width of cable A (center panel)	____ inches (cm)	**3½** inches	Width of **center panel cable A**.
Width of cable B	____ inches (cm)	**1** inch	Width of **side cable B**.
Width of cable C	____ inches (cm)	**4** inches	Width of **side cable C**.
	Same information for each individual **cable pattern**.		
Cable panel widths *Planning for cable sequence across the width of the poncho*	Cable B Cable C Cable B Cable A (center) Cable B Cable C Cable B	Cable B = 1 inch Cable C = 4 inches Cable B = 1 inch Cable A = 3½ inches Cable B = 1 inch Cable C = 4 inches Cable B = 1 inch	To determine the width of the poncho pieces, you need to have a total for the **cable panel widths.** If you will use any cables more than once, make sure you list them as many times as necessary. Don't forget to include any plain stitches you plan to use between the cables. Use separate paper if necessary.

Worksheet continues on next page

Gauge measurements for project 7 (continued)

	Calculation	Example	Description
Total width of cables	____ inches (cm)	**15½ inches**	Add the widths of all the cable panels (and plain stitches, if added). This is the **total width of all the cable panels**.
Total width of side stitch area	____ – ____ = ____ inches (cm)	21 – 15½ = **5½ inches**	Subtract the total width of all the cable panels from the width of one poncho piece to determine how much of the **width will be filled with the side stitch**.
Side stitch panel width	____ ÷ 2 = ____ inches (cm)	5½ ÷ 2 = **2¾ inches**	Divide the total width of the side stitch area by 2 to determine the **width of the side stitch panel** that you will have on each side of the poncho pieces.

Stitch counts for project 7

	Calculation	Example	Description
Side stitches	____ x ____ = ____	2¾ x 5 = **13.75** **14 stitches**	Multiply the side-stitch width by your stitch gauge to calculate the **number of side stitches.** If your answer is a fraction, round up to the nearest whole stitch.
Cable panel stitches	Cable B ____ + Cable C ____ + Cable B ____ + Cable A (center) ____ + Cable B ____ + Cable C ____ + Cable B ____ = ____ stitches	Cable B = 9 sts Cable C = 15 sts Cable B = 9 sts Cable A = 24 sts Cable B = 9 sts Cable C = 15 sts Cable B = 9 sts = **90 stitches**	Add up the number of stitches in all of the cable panels. Refer to your swatches and your planning sketch to make sure you include all of the cables. Don't forget to include any plain stitches you plan to use between the cables. Use separate paper if necessary.
Main number of stitches	____ + ____ + ____ = ____ stitches	14 + 14 + 90 = **118 stitches**	Add the side stitches (for both sides) to the cable panel stitches to determine the **main number of stitches**, or total number of stitches for each poncho piece.

Abbreviation
sts = stitches

Need a slightly different stitch count? Increase or decrease by a few.

Knit! *option 3: a step-by-step project sheet*

Ireland
Poncho

Do the calculations on the planning worksheet above so you have the numbers to fill in here.

1 Cast on

Cast on ____ stitches (**main number of stitches**). Work back and forth.

2 Knit the cable panels

Set up patterns, placing a marker between each pattern and the next, as follows:

Work ____ **side stitches** in side stitch pattern, place marker, *work stitches for cable pattern, place marker, repeat from * until all cable panels have been set up, work last ____ **side stitches** in side stitch pattern.

Work even in patterns as established until piece measures ____ inches (cm) (**length**) from cast-on edge.

Bind off loosely.

Repeat steps 1 and 2 for second piece.

3 Finish

Sew pieces together as shown in diagram on page 136. One short end of each piece is sewn to one long end of the other, matching the corners. Because the cables will cause the short ends to draw in, you may find it easiest to make a neat seam of you wash the pieces and lay them flat to dry before seaming.

Weave in the ends.

Aran Pullovers with Saddle Shoulders

I've designed two different Aran pullovers, but the basic instructions for both are the same. In the simpler and easier sweater, I designed the body using just two cables, and the sleeves have only a single, centered rope cable surrounded by moss stitch. The second sweater is slightly more complicated, with more cable patterns on the body and the sleeves. I also threw in a few bobbles for good measure.

You'll notice that the sweater-planning worksheets for the Aran sweaters are quite long. However, the line-by-line instructions are much shorter than for other types of sweaters. All of the hard work is in the planning—really!

Even though the basic instructions for sweaters 8 and 9 are the same, I have given the two projects separate planning worksheets and have included sample swatches as a reminder of how important it is to test out all the patterns you will use.

- ☑ Cable and texture patterning
- ☑ Worked back and forth in pieces, with saddle shoulders
- ☑ Sleeves worked from cuffs up to saddles and sewn into place

Both sweater examples have been designed in worsted-weight yarn with a moss stitch (side pattern stitch) gauge of 5 stitches and 6 rows to the inch (20 stitches and 24 rows to 10 cm). They also both have a 40-inch (102-cm) body circumference and 24-inch (61-cm) body length (including 2 inches [5 cm] of ribbing). The sweater on the left is simpler, with only two cable patterns in addition to the moss-stitch filler. The sweater on the right incorporates more complex cable patterns. See the worksheets for specific information on patterns.

Get ready   *yarn & needles*

Yarn

As for the poncho (project 7), a smooth, dense yarn will show off the cable patterns best. Tightly spun yarns make the cable patterns pop out from the background, while softly spun yarns result in softer cable definition and a fabric that retains drape.

When knitting for children, I always choose a machine-washable yarn. Good choices for cable knitting include superwash wool or blends of wool with acrylic or cotton.

You can knit Arans with 100 percent cotton yarn, although I don't like to use cotton for cables because the yarn has so little give that it's difficult to cross the stitches.

Aran sweaters are frequently made with what is called Aran-weight yarn, which knits up at about 4½ stitches per inch (18 stitches to 10 cm). Worsted-weight yarn (5 stitches per inch or 20 stitches per 10 cm) is a close second. You can make a gorgeous heirloom sweater by knitting an Aran pattern with light- or fine-weight yarn, but practice with a heavier yarn first! Bulky yarns are sometimes used by fashion designers to create funky sweaters that look good on a runway, but these will likely be hot and heavy to wear for those of us who do not live in Arctic climates.

For practice, I suggest a medium-weight yarn and U.S. size 7 or 8 (4.5 or 5 mm) knitting needles.

Yarn guidelines, including a yardage estimate table, are on pages 20–22. Increase the estimates by about 30 percent for a densely cabled sweater.

Knitting needles

In a size appropriate for the yarn you've chosen:

✦ Straight or circular needle(s) for body and sleeves; because you will work back and forth, the length of the circular needle is not critical

Two sizes smaller than primary needles:

✦ Straight or circular needle(s) for ribbings

✦ Circular needle(s) for neckband: 16 inches (40 cm) long

If you want to knit your Aran sweater in the round, see pages 160–161 for instructions and pages 18–20 for tips on choosing circular needle lengths and working small tubes on circular needles.

Additional supplies

✦ Stitch markers

★ Projects 8 and 9 share instructions EXCEPT for their gauge and stitch-count worksheets.

★ Project 8, simpler version, uses gauge and stitch count worksheets on pages 148–151.

★ Project 9, more complex version, uses gauge and stitch count worksheets on pages 152–156.

★ Make your version as simple or complex as you like.

Cover sweater story: Aran-style cardigan for an adult   *by Debbie O'Neill*

I love Aran knitting, especially sweaters. When Donna asked me to work up an Aran sweater design using this book, I didn't even have a moment's hesitation. In my mind, I saw a saddle-shouldered cardigan that had overall patterning, but clean, simple lines. I picked the Aran diamonds as the primary motif to work around. I decided to highlight the diamonds with rope cables and little O-shaped cables.

Because cables can change the gauge of your knitting significantly compared to stockinette stitch, I was careful to swatch all of the pattern stitches I planned to use in the cardigan. I also found it helpful to sketch out the motifs in a single chart so that I had an idea of what the finished sweater would look like before I started knitting. Drawing out a single chart makes it easier to visualize details, like the mirroring I did with the rope cables on either side of the diamonds.

Once I had all my stitch motifs figured out, I did some math to figure out how much filler—for example, reverse stockinette stitch around the cables—I needed to add

to end up with the right size of sweater. Because of varying cable gauges, this was not as simple as just figuring out a stitch gauge and multiplying by the number of inches to know how many stitches to cast on. I figured out the stitch count and gauge for each cable I planned on using and determined how many inches and stitches they would contribute to the project. Then I made up the difference with moss stitch and reverse stockinette stitch to get the right finished size. I started the knitting with one cardigan front, which allowed me to sanity-check my plan.

The sleeves are simple—they fit into the modified drop-shoulder armhole of this sweater shape and include a shoulder saddle. The central cable motif is carried across the saddle. I knitted the saddles, then sewed them to the fronts and back of the sweater. I could have knitted each saddle to the garment as I worked it, but I think sewing makes the shoulder seams firmer, and I like that extra stability. The neckband and button bands are just a small amount of garter stitch. I wanted them to be subtle.

Get set   *stitches, gauge & size*

Stitches and gauge

▌ Select the ribbing, cable panels, and side stitch for your sweater. Use a combination shown in the illustration on page 140 (and in the examples on pages 148 or 152–153) or choose your own combination of stitches, either from this book or from a knitting-stitch library.

When you are selecting cables, remember that the sweater will have one main center panel, surrounded by other cables that are mirror images on either side of that panel. The sleeve will also have a center panel. This may be the same as the center panel on the body, or you may decide to use a narrower panel on the sleeve. Make sure the panel you choose for the center of the sleeve will fit in the width of the saddle shoulder.

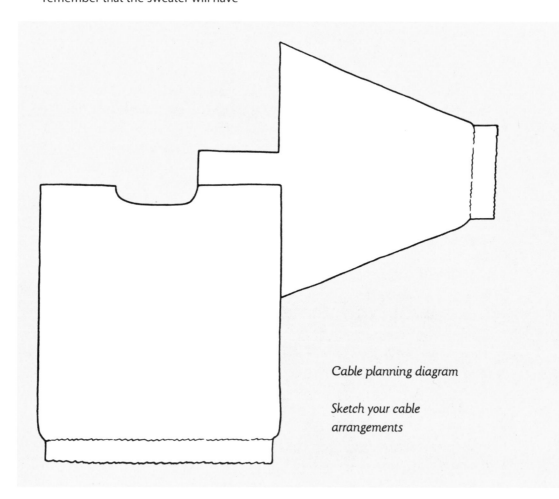

Cable planning diagram

Sketch your cable arrangements

Sketch the arrangement of your cable panels on a blank sweater-planning diagram, like the one on the previous page. The front and back will have the same pattern sequence, so you only need to sketch in the front, although the front will have neck shaping and the back will not.

2 Make a gauge swatch in moss stitch or the side stitch of your choice.

3 Measure your gauge. Write the stitch gauge and row gauge on the sweater-planning worksheet on page 148 (project 8) or 152 (project 9).

4 Knit a swatch of each cable panel. If you are using small patterns, you may decide to knit these on the sides of a larger cable instead of making a separate swatch for each pattern.

Place the cable swatches on a flat surface to see how you like the arrangement of the stitches. Redo your cable planning sketch if necessary.

5 Measure the width of each cable panel and estimate how many panels you will need for the desired width. Make sure you don't measure the border on the sides of your swatch, although you may want to include enough plain stitches to clearly define the pattern.

Record the cable width measurements on the sweater-planning worksheets (pages 148–149 for project 8; pages 152 and 154 for project 9) and check to see

if these add up to the desired measurement for the sweater width.

6 Knit a swatch of the combined cable patterns and side stitch for half of the back plus the center panel of your sweater.

Step 6 is optional, but I never skip it. It helps me see what the entire sweater will look like and lets me practice knitting the combination of cables together. Sometimes I change my mind about aspects of the design at this stage, including whether or not I want plain stitches between my cable panels.

Size

1 Measure your favorite sweater or use the size charts on page 16 to determine the basic dimensions for your sweater. Write the measurements on the visual plan on page 146 and the sweater-planning worksheet on page 147.

2 Use the calculations on the worksheets (pages 150–151 for project 8; pages 155–156 for project 9) to figure all the remaining numbers before you start, or just calculate each new number as you need it.

3 Transfer the resulting numbers to the visual plan on page 146 or the step-by-step instructions on pages 157–159, depending on how much guiding detail you would like to have while you knit.

Knit! *option I: using a visual plan*

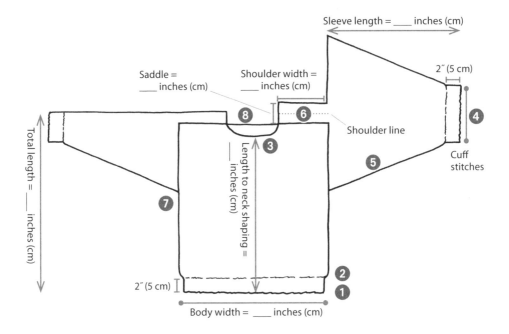

Sleeve length = ____ inches (cm)

2″ (5 cm)

Saddle =
____ inches (cm)

Shoulder width =
____ inches (cm)

4

Cuff
stitches

8 **6**

Shoulder line

Total length = ____ inches (cm)

Length to neck shaping = ____ inches (cm)

3

5

7

2″ (5 cm)

2
1

Body width = ____ inches (cm)

BACK

1 Cast on ____ stitches (stitches to cast on) and knit ribbing

2 Increase to ____ stitches (main number of stitches) and set up cable patterns; work back and forth to length-to-saddle (no neck shaping), and bind off

FRONT

Work steps **1** and **2** as for back until you reach the length where you will begin the front neck shaping

3 Work neck shaping and bind off shoulders

SLEEVES

4 Cast on ____ cuff stitches and knit ribbing

5 Change to cable patterns; increase at even intervals along underarm to ____ sleeve stitches; knit to sleeve length and bind off all stitches but saddle

6 Knit saddle and bind off

FINISH

7 Sew seams

8 Work neckband ribbing, bind off, and weave in ends

Knit! *option 2: using planning worksheets*

Ireland
Aran Sweater

Sweater measurements (for both projects 8 and 9)

	Calculation	Example	Description
Gauge measurements are recorded on pages 150 and 152.			
Body width	___ inches (cm)	**20** inches	Measure the **width** of the sweater body.
Body circumference	___ × 2 = ___ inches	20 × 2 = **40** inches	Double the body width for the **circumference of the sweater**. This is the finished chest/bust size.
Total length	___ inches (cm)	**24** inches	Measure the **total length** of the sweater body.
Sleeve length	___ inches (cm)	**18** inches	Measure the **sleeve length** from wrist to underarm.
Armhole depth	___ ÷ 2 = ___ inches	20 ÷ 2 = **10** inches	Divide the body width by 2 to calculate the **armhole depth**.
Neck width	___ ÷ 3 = ___ inches	20 ÷ 3 = **6⅔** inches	Measure the neck on your sample sweater, or divide the body width in thirds, or use the sweater proportion diagram on page 15 to determine the **width of the neck opening**.
Sleeve circumference	___ × 2 = ___ inches	10 × 2 = **20** inches	Double the armhole depth for the **circumference of the sleeve** at the shoulder.
Saddle width	___ inches (cm)	**3** inches	The center cable on the sleeve extends to the neckline to form the saddle shoulder. The **saddle width** should not be more than 2 inches (5 cm) for children or 4 inches (10 cm) for adults.
Length of front & back to saddle	___ − (½ x ___) = ___ inches	24 − 1½ = **22½** inches	Subtract ½ of the saddle width from the total length to determine the **length to the saddle** on the front and back.
Begin front neck shaping	3 inches − (½ × ___) = ___ inches ___ − ___ = ___ inches	3 − 1½ = **1½** inches 22½ − 1½ = **21** inches	Subtract ½ of the saddle width from 3 inches (7.5 cm). Subtract this result from the length to saddle to determine where to **begin front neck shaping** for an average neck depth of 3 inches (7.5 cm).

A
B
C
D

Gauge information for project 8

	Calculation	Example	Description
Stitch gauge for side stitch	____ stitches = 1 inch or 1 cm	**5** stitches = 1 inch	**Stitch gauge** is critical for knitting a sweater that fits properly.
Width of cable A (center panel)	____ inches (cm)	**9** inches	Width of **center panel cable A**. Calculate from swatch along with desired number of repeats within panel.
Width of cable B	____ inches (cm)	**1¼** inches	Width of **side cable B**.
Gather the same information for each individual cable pattern.			

Example

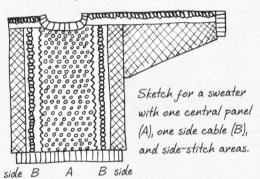

Sketch for a sweater with one central panel (A), one side cable (B), and side-stitch areas.

side B   A   B side

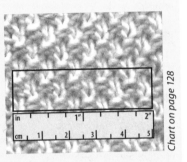

Chart on page 128

Side stitch = moss stitch

5 stitches per inch
(20 stitches to 10 cm)

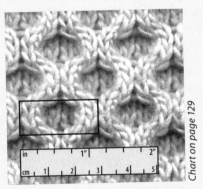

Chart on page 129

Center panel (A) = 8-stitch honeycomb by 8 repeats

One 8-stitch repeat = 1⅛ inches (2.9 cm)
8 repeats = 64 stitches and 9 inches (22.9 cm)

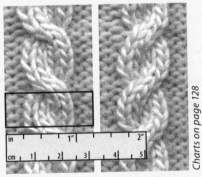

Charts on page 128

Side cable (B) = 6-stitch rope cables set off by reverse stockinette

One 6-stitch cable with 2 reverse stockinette stitches on each side = 10 stitches and 1¼ inches (3.2 cm)

Pattern area measurements for project 8

	Calculation	Example	Description
Body: Cable panel widths	plain ___ + Cable B = ___ inches plain ___ + Cable A (center) = ___ inches plain ___ + Cable B = ___ inches plain ___ +	½ inch plain Cable B = 1¼ inches ½ inch plain Cable A = 9 inches ½ inch plain Cable B = 1¼ inches ½ inch plain	**Cable panel widths** are used along with gauge to calculate the width of the sweater. If you will use any cables more than once, make sure you list them as many times as necessary. Don't forget to include any plain areas you plan to use between the cables. In this case, the plain areas will be reverse stockinette stitch. Use separate paper to sketch out your arrangement and calculations if you like.
Body: Total combined width of cable panels	___ + ___ + ___ = ___ inches (cm)	½ + 1¼ + ½ + 9 + ½ + 1¼ + ½ = **13½** inches	Add the widths of all the cable panels (and plain areas, if included). This is the **total combined width of the cable panels** for the body.
Body: Total width of side stitch area	___ – ___ = ___ inches (cm)	20 – 13½ = **6½** inches	Subtract the total combined width of the cable panels from the sweater width to determine how much of the **body width will be filled with the side stitch**.
Body: Side stitch panel width	___ ÷ 2 = ___ inches (cm)	6½ ÷ 2 = **3¼** inches	Divide the total width of the side stitch area by 2 to determine the **width of the side stitch panel** that you will have on each side of the body front and back pieces. If the math starts getting too precise, fudge.
Sleeve: Center panel width	___ inches (cm)	**2 inches** The panel is 2 inches wide. The cable in the example is 1¼ inches wide. The remaining panel width can be filled with plain stitches.	The center cable on the sleeve extends to the neckline to form the saddle shoulder. This **sleeve center panel width** should not be greater than 2 inches (5 cm) for children or 4 inches (10 cm) for adults.

Stitch counts for project 8

	Calculation	Example	Description
a Side stitches	× ____ = ____ stitches	3¼ × 5 = **15¾** **16** stitches	Multiply the side-stitch width by your stitch gauge to calculate the **number of side stitches.** If your answer is a fraction, round up or down to the nearest whole stitch.
Cable panel stitches	plain ____ + Cable B ____ + plain ____ + Cable A ____ + plain ____ + Cable B ____ + plain ____ = ____ stitches	plain = 3 stitches Cable B = 10 stitches plain = 2 stitches Cable A = 64 stitches plain = 2 stitches Cable B = 10 stitches plain = 3 stitches = **94 stitches**	Add up the number of stitches in all of the cable panels. Refer to your swatches and your planning sketch to make sure you include all of the cables. Don't forget to include any plain stitches you plan to use between the cables. Use separate paper if necessary.
b Main number of stitches	____ + ____ + ____ = ____ stitches	16 + 16 + 94 = **126 stitches**	Add the side stitches (for both sides) to the cable panel stitches to determine the **main number of stitches**, or total number of stitches for each body piece (front and back).
c Stitches to cast on	____ × .9 = ____ stitches	126 × .9 = **113.4 stitches** 112 stitches (multiple of 4) 114 stitches (multiple of 4, plus 2)	Multiply the main number of stitches by .9 (90 percent) to calculate the number of stitches to cast on for ribbing. *But see note about cables and gauge and stitch counts on pages 122–123.* Round up or down to the nearest multiple of your ribbing pattern. Remember that because you are knitting your pieces flat, you will want to center the ribbing. For example, for k2, p2 ribbing, you need a multiple of 4 stitches plus 2.

Stitch counts for project 8 (continued)

		Calculation	Example	Description
d	*Neck stitches & Shoulder stitches*	____ stitches for neck ____ stitches for each shoulder	Approximately **42** stitches for neck Approximately **42** stitches for each shoulder Numbers will vary because of the different gauges of the panels. Rely on the measurements, as noted in the description.	When you have knitted the front up to the point where you will begin the neck shaping, mark the location of the front neck based on your neck width measurements. Use safety pins. Count the number of **neck stitches** between the markers. Count the number of stitches remaining in each shoulder. Make sure you have the same number of **shoulder stitches** on each side. Adjust the number of neck stitches if necessary to even out the shoulders.
e	*Cuff stitches*	____ stitches	**40** stitches 40 stitches is a multiple of 4 **42** stitches (multiple of 4, plus 2)	After you knit the body of your sweater, wrap the ribbing of one of the pieces around your wrist to a snugness level that feels right and use that section of fabric as a reference to count the **number of stitches for the cuff**. Round up or down to a multiple of your chosen ribbing. Remember that because you are knitting your pieces flat, you will want to center the ribbing. For example, for k2, p2 ribbing, you need a multiple of 4 stitches plus 2.
f	*Neck bind-off stitches*	____ × 2½ = ____ stitches ____ − ____ = ____ stitches	5 × 2½ = 12½ stitches 42 − 12½ = **29½** stitches Rounded to **30** stitches	Multiply your gauge by 2½ inches (6.5 cm). Subtract this number of stitches from the neck stitches for the number of **stitches to bind off at the beginning of the neck shaping** on the front. If your sweater front has an even number of stitches, round the result to an even number; if your sweater front has an odd number of stitches, round it to an odd number.

Need a slightly different stitch count? Increase or decrease by a few.

This example has been set up with numbers that clearly demonstrate the simple calculations. Those numbers happen to result in an adult's sweater with a finished chest measurement of 40″ (102 cm) that falls to a generous hip length. If you're not that size, and few of us will be, use the guidelines on pages 14–17 and measurements you gather for yourself to make a sweater that is customized for its wearer.

Gauge information for project 9

	Calculation	Example	Description
Stitch gauge for side stitch	____ stitches = 1 inch or 1 cm	**5** stitches = 1 inch	**Stitch gauge** is critical for knitting a sweater that fits properly.
Width of cable A (center panel)	____ inches (cm)	**2¾** inches	Width of **center panel cable A**. Calculate from swatch along with desired number of repeats within panel.
Width of cable B	____ inches (cm)	**⅝** inch 3 repeats = 3 × ⅝ = **1⅞** inches	Width of **side cable B** (one repeat); patterns with narrow repeats offer design flexibility.
Width of cable C	____ inches (cm)	**2¾** inches	Width of **side cable C**. In this case, C is the same as A. It doesn't have to be. And you can have even more patterns.
Gather the same information for each individual cable pattern; the examples for project 9 are provided in less detail than the examples for project 8.			

Example

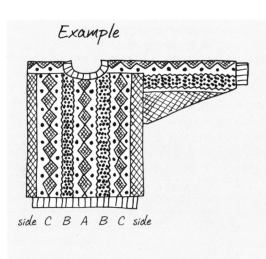

side C B A B C side

Sketch for a sweater with one central panel (A), two side panels (B & C), and side-stitch areas.

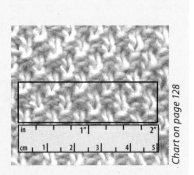

Chart on page 128

Side stitch = moss stitch

5 stitches per inch
(20 stitches to 10 cm)

Example

 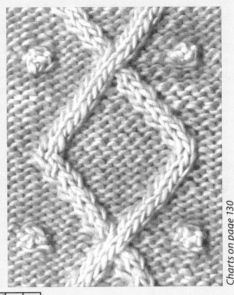

Charts on page 130

Center cable A and side cables C = Diamonds with bobbles

One repeat = 2¾ inches (7 cm), including 1 extra stitch of reverse stockinette on each edge

As a side cable, the pattern above can be right-crossing on one side of the sweater and left-crossing on the other. As a center cable, you can choose either crossing, or you can alternate the crossings.

The cable pattern below is very flexible. You can choose the number of repeats to fit the available space, and fill any gaps with plain stitches.

Side cable B = 4-stitch honeycomb

One repeat = ⅝ inch (1.6 cm)
Multiples:

    2 repeats = 1¼ inches (3.2 cm)
    3 repeats = 1⅞ inches (4.8 cm)
    4 repeats = 2½ inches (6.4 cm)
    5 repeats = 3⅛ inches (7.9 cm)
    6 repeats = 3¾ inches (9.5 cm)
    7 repeats = 4⅜ inches (11.1 cm)
    8 repeats = 5 inches (12.7 cm)

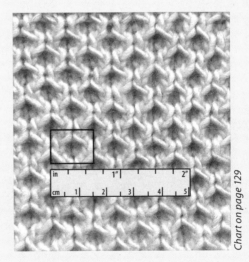

Chart on page 129

Pattern area measurements for project 9

	Calculation	Example	Description
Body: Cable panel widths	plain ____ + Cable C = ____ inches plain ____ + Cable B = ____ inches plain ____ + Cable A (center) = ____ inches plain ____ + Cable B = ____ inches plain ____ + Cable C = ____ inches plain ____ +	½ inch plain Cable C = 2¾ inches ½ inch plain Cable B = 1⅞ inches ½ inch plain Cable A = 2¾ inches ½ inch plain Cable B = 1⅞ inches ½ inch plain Cable C = 2¾ inches ½ inch plain	**Cable panel widths** are used along with gauge to calculate the width of the sweater. If you will use any cables more than once, make sure you list them as many times as necessary. Don't forget to include any plain stitches you plan to use between the cables. Use separate paper to sketch out your arrangement and calculations if you like.
Body: Total combined width of cable panels	____ inches (cm)	**15** inches	Add the widths of all the cable panels (and plain stitches, if added). This is the **total width of all the cable panels for the body**.
Body: Total width of side stitch area	____ − ____ = ____ inches (cm)	20 − 15 = **5** inches	Subtract the total combined width of the cable panels from the sweater width to determine how much of the **body width will be filled with the side stitch area**.
Body: Side stitch panel width	____ ÷ 2 = ____ inches (cm)	5 ÷ 2 = **2½** inches	Divide the total width of the side stitch area by 2 to determine the **width of the side stitch panel** on each side of the body front and back pieces.
Sleeve: Center panel width	____ inches (cm)	**4** inches The panel is 4 inches wide. The cable in the example is 2¾ inches wide. Fill the remaining 1¼ inches with plain stitches.	The center cable on the sleeve extends to the neckline to form the saddle shoulder. This **sleeve center panel width** should not be greater than 2 inches (5 cm) for children or 4 inches (10 cm) for adults.

Stitch counts for project 9

	Calculation	Example	Description
a Side stitches	____ × ____ = ____ stitches	2½ × 5 = **12½** stitches **13** stitches	Multiply the side-stitch width by your stitch gauge to calculate the **number of side stitches.** If your answer is a fraction, round up to the nearest whole stitch.
Cable panel stitches	plain ____ + Cable C ____ + plain ____ + Cable B ____ + plain ____ + Cable A ____ + plain ____ + Cable B ____ + plain ____ + Cable C ____ + plain ____ =____ stitches	plain = 3 stitches Cable C = 14 stitches plain = 2 stitches Cable B = 12 stitches plain = 2 stitches Cable A =14 stitches plain = 2 stitches Cable B = 12 stitches plain = 2 stitches Cable C = 14 stitches plain = 3 stitches = **80** stitches	Add up the number of stitches in all of the cable panels. Refer to your swatches and your planning sketch to make sure you include all of the cables. Don't forget to include any plain stitches you plan to use between the cables. Use separate paper if necessary.
b Main number of stitches	____ + ____ + ____ = ____ stitches	13 + 13 + 80 = **106** stitches	Add the side stitches (for both sides) to the cable panel stitches to determine the **main number of stitches**, or total number of stitches for each body piece (front and back).
c Stitches to cast on	____ × .9 = ____ stitches	106 × .9 = **95.4** stitches 96 stitches (multiple of 4) 98 stitches (multiple of 4, plus 2)	Multiply the main number of stitches by 90 percent to calculate the number of stitches to cast on for ribbing. *But see note about cables and gauge and stitch counts on pages 122–123.* Round up or down to the nearest multiple of your ribbing pattern. Remember that because you are knitting your pieces flat, you will want to center the ribbing. For example, for k2, p2 ribbing, you need a multiple of 4 stitches plus 2.

Worksheet continues on next page

Stitch counts for project 9 (continued)

		Calculation	Example	Description
d	Neck stitches & Shoulder stitches	____ stitches for neck ____ stitches for each shoulder	Approximately **36** stitches for neck Approximately **35** stitches for each shoulder Numbers will vary because of the different gauges of the panels. Rely on the measurements, as noted in the description.	When you have knitted the front up to the point where you will begin the neck shaping, mark the location of the front neck based on your measurements. Use safety pins. Count the number of **neck stitches** between the markers. Count the number of stitches remaining in each shoulder. Make sure you have the same number of **shoulder stitches** on each side. Adjust the number of neck stitches if necessary to even out the shoulders.
e	Cuff stitches	____ stitches	**40** stitches 40 stitches is a multiple of 4 42 stitches (multiple of 4, plus 2)	After you knit the body of your sweater, wrap the ribbing of one of the pieces around your wrist to a snugness level that feels right and use that section of fabric as a reference to count the **number of stitches for the cuff**. Round up or down to a multiple of your chosen ribbing. Remember that because you are knitting your pieces flat, you will want to center the ribbing. For example, for k2, p2 ribbing, you need a multiple of 4 stitches plus 2.
f	Neck bind-off stitches	____ × 2½ = ____ stitches ____ − ____ = ____ stitches	$5 \times 2\frac{1}{2} = 12\frac{1}{2}$ stitches $36 - 12\frac{1}{2} = $ **23 ½** stitches Rounded to **24** stitches	Multiply your gauge by 2½ inches (6.5 cm). Subtract this number of stitches from the neck stitches for the number of **stitches to bind off at the beginning of the neck shaping** on the front. If your sweater front has an even number of stitches, round the result to an even number; if your sweater front has an odd number of stitches, round it to an odd number.

Need a slightly different stitch count? Increase or decrease by a few.

This example has been set up with numbers that clearly demonstrate the simple calculations. Those numbers happen to result in an adult's sweater with a finished chest measurement of 40″ (102 cm) that falls to a generous hip length. If you're not that size, and few of us will be, use the guidelines on pages 14–17 and measurements you gather for yourself to make a sweater that is customized for its wearer.

Knit!   *option 3: a step-by-step project sheet*   Ireland
Aran Sweater

Use this project sheet if you are not yet comfortable working directly from the sweater-planning diagram. With time, you'll find that you no longer need to refer to these instructions.

Do the calculations on the planning worksheets on pages 148–151 (project 8) or 152–156 (project 9) so you have the numbers to fill in here.

BACK

1 Cast on and knit ribbing

With the smaller circular needle, cast on ____ stitches (**stitches to cast on**). Remember, you are working the front and back separately so do not join.

Work back and forth in your chosen ribbing until the piece measures 2 inches (5 cm), or until ribbing is desired length. End after completing a wrong-side row.

On the next right-side row, increase to ____ stitches (**main number of stitches**) as follows, working the ribbing pattern as established:

If all of your cables are approximately the same density, *K9, increase 1, repeat from * to end of row.

If some of your cables are denser than others, work the same total number of increases in the row but position more increases in the areas of the dense cables

and fewer increases in the areas of the lighter cables. (See pages 122–127.)

2 Work cable panels

Change to main needle.

Work ____ **side stitches** in side-stitch pattern, place a marker (pm), *work stitches for cable pattern, pm; repeat from * for all cable panels to last ____ **side stitches**, then work remaining stitches in side-stitch pattern.

Work even in patterns as established until the piece measures ____ inches (cm) (**length to saddle**) from the cast-on edge.

Bind off.

FRONT

Repeat steps 1 and 2, same as for back, until piece measures ____ inches (cm) (**begin neck shaping**).

3 Shape neckline

Bind off the center ____ **neck bind-off stitches.**

Work the shoulders separately, or work them at the same time using separate balls of yarn. On each of the next several right-side rows, bind off 2 stitches at the neck edge until ____ stitches (**shoulder stitches**) remain on each side. Work even, if necessary, until the front is the same length as the back.

Note: This simplified neck shaping has a wide flat area in the center and small curves at the corners. It will work beautifully in medium- and lightweight yarns. For heavier yarns, bind off fewer stitches in the center, and work fewer rows of decreases. Don't worry about this too much; just bind off enough to reach the number of shoulder stitches on each side. When you add the neck-band, it will help smooth out the curvature of the neckline.

d   Bind off ____ **shoulder stitches** on each side.

SLEEVES

4   **Cast on and knit cuffs**

e   With double-pointed needles, cast on ____ **cuff stitches**. Do not join (unless you are working circularly). Work back and forth in your chosen ribbing until the piece measures 2 inches (5 cm), or until ribbing is desired length. End after completing a wrong-side row.

On the next right-side row, set up for cables as for body.

5   **Begin sleeve increases**

Change to main needle and pattern stitches of your choice.

AT THE SAME TIME, begin increasing for the sleeve as follows: On every 4th

round, knit 1, increase 1, work in pattern to the last stitch, increase 1, knit 1. Work increases into side-stitch pattern.

Keep an eye on the shape of your sleeve and measure it against your model sweater or try your sleeve on after every few inches (cm) to make sure the sleeve is increasing at a comfortable rate. If your sleeve is becoming wide too quickly, start increasing every 6th row. If it is not widening fast enough, start increasing every 3rd row.

Tip: I don't count stitches when increasing a sleeve on an Aran-style sweater. I just work until the sleeve is the width and length that I need. See pages 122–123 for information on measuring cables.

Continue increasing until the sleeve is ____ inches (cm) wide (**sleeve circumference)** and then work even until the sleeve is ____ inches (cm) long (**sleeve length**).

6   **Knit saddle and bind off sleeve**

Bind off all stitches except for the saddle.

Continue to work back and forth on the center panel until the saddle length equals the width of the front shoulder.

Bind off the remaining stitches.

Make second sleeve the same way as the first, steps 4 through 6.

FINISH

Sew seams

Using the sweater-planning diagram as a guide, sew the sweater together:

☆ Sew the saddles to the shoulders on the front and back.

☆ Sew the sleeves to the body.

☆ Sew the side and underarm seams.

Neckband

Using a 16-inch (40-cm) circular needle (in a slightly smaller size, if you like) and starting at the left shoulder with the right side of the sweater facing you, pick up stitches down the left side of the neck front, across the front stitches that you bound off, up the right side of the neck front, and across the back stitches that you bound off. Pick up the stitches at about a 1-for-1 ratio with your edge and make sure you have the correct multiple for your chosen ribbing. See pages 122–123 for more information on cables, gauge, and stitch counts.

Work in ribbing, in the round, until the neckband measures 1 inch (2.5 cm). Bind off loosely in pattern.

Weave in the ends.

Transatlantic traditions?

One theory of the development of the Aran sweater suggests that an Irish woman got the idea for knitting the dense cable patterns during a visit to America, where she met a knitter who may have been from Scandinavia or Central Europe, where textured knitting was very common. Although we'll probably never know if this story is true, it does show how knitting patterns and sweater designs can quickly travel around the globe and how techniques from different regions influence each other in surprising ways. Aran knitting made its way into the mainstream consciousness of U.S. knitters when Elizabeth Zimmermann designed an Aran sweater for *Vogue Knitting* in 1958.

Knitting Arans in the round

Although I prefer to make Aran sweaters flat in pieces because I think it is much easier, I know some knitters prefer to knit all sweaters circularly. Here is a short work plan for knitting an Aran sweater in the round. I trust that you have a good bit of circular knitting under your belt before you try this!

 Work the body

Cast on the back stitches, place a marker, cast on the front stitches, place another marker, then join to knit in the round.

Work the ribbing and set up the cable patterns between the markers for the front and the back just as for flat knitting. When you work every round on the right side, remember to read all chart rows from right to left.

At the armholes, separate for back and front. Starting at the beginning of the round, knit across the back stitches to the first marker. The stitches you have just knitted will be used for the upper back. Place the front stitches on hold for knitting the upper front. Work the upper back and upper front just as for knitting the sweater flat.

Note: If you are going to knit the sleeves from the shoulder down, do not bind off the shoulder stitches on the front or back of the body.

2 **Work the sleeves**

Sleeves can be worked from the cuff up and sewn in or worked from the saddle shoulder down without seams.

Sleeve option 1: Cuff-up

Cast on as for a flat sleeve, then place a marker and join to knit in the round.

Use double-pointed needles or see pages 18–20 for tips on choosing circular needle lengths and working small tubes on circular needles.

Work the sleeve increases on either side of the marker instead of at the beginning and end of rows.

When the sleeve is the desired length, bind off all the stitches except the saddle (center panel) stitches. Work back and forth in pattern on these stitches until the saddle is the same length as the front shoulder width.

Sew the sides of the saddle to the front and back shoulders, then sew the sleeve into the armhole.

Sleeve option 2: Shoulder-down

This technique is quite complicated and not recommended for new knitters. This only works if your cable patterns look the same right-side-up and upside-down. If you are brave enough to try this,

I trust that you have the skills to work out the numbers on your own.

Put the center back neck stitches on a holder if they have not been bound off. The front neck stitches have been bound off during neck shaping. Double check to make sure you have the same number of stitches in the front and back shoulders.

Work the attached saddle. Using a double-pointed needle, cast on the required number of stitches for the saddle, plus 2 extra stitches. Work as follows, beginning at the neck:

Row 1 (right side): Slip 1 as if to knit. Work cable pattern to last stitch. SSK, working the last stitch of the saddle together with first stitch at the edge of the shoulder. Turn.

Row 2 (wrong side): Slip 1 as if to purl with the yarn in front. Work cable pattern to last stitch. P2tog, combining the last stitch of the saddle with the first stitch at the edge of the shoulder. Turn.

Repeat rows 1 and 2, working each decrease with the next live stitch at the adjacent shoulder edge until the saddle has been attached to the entire shoulder.

Pick up stitches around the armhole, remembering that you will need to increase on the first row wherever you will be placing a cable so the fabric won't pucker. (See pages 122–127 for more information on this.)

Tip: See pages 18–20 for tips on choosing the circular needle lengths and working small tubes on circular needles.

Work the remainder of the sleeve as for a flat sleeve, but instead of increasing on both sides of the marker, decrease. Change to double-pointed needles when your stitches no longer fit comfortably on the circular needle. When the sleeve has the correct number of stitches for the cuff and is the desired length, work the cuff and bind off very loosely.

3 Finishing

Work the neckband as for the flat sweater and weave in the ends.

Cardigans

There are three different ways to work cardigans:

◆ You can work the sweater in the round and then cut the front open;

◆ You can work the body back and forth as one piece with the opening at the center front; or

◆ You can work the entire sweater in pieces and sew them together.

I find that each of these techniques comes in handy for different types of sweaters. My preferences for when to choose each technique are summarized in the table on page 165. You may find that your preferences are different. Give each of these alternatives a try and see what works best for you.

In the round with a cut center-front opening

This is the ideal technique for when you are working with multiple colors, because the front side of the fabric always faces you and you can watch your color patterning develop—plus, of course, you don't have to keep track of two or more colors while purling. It's also great for simple sweaters because you can go on knitting autopilot until it's time to finish the garment.

To knit a cardigan in the round, create a steek at the center front by casting on 3, 5, or 7 extra stitches. Place a marker on the center steek stitch to indicate the beginning of the round. Beginners, or anyone who is experimenting with steeks worked in yarns other than wool, should start with 7 stitches.

As you continue on the following rows, work the steek stitches in stockinette stitch, using a simple alternating

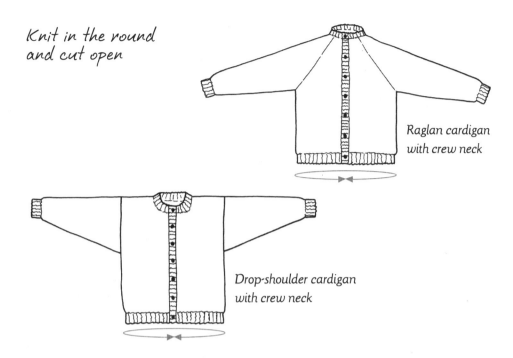

Knit in the round and cut open

Raglan cardigan
with crew neck

Drop-shoulder cardigan
with crew neck

color pattern, like those shown on the opposite page, if you are working with more than one color. Be sure to secure all the colors in each row within the steek.

When you are finished knitting the sweater body, run a line or two of hand or machine stitching on either side of the column of stitches that you will cut to make the opening. Then snip through that center column of stitches with sharp sewing shears. Fold the steek back

Stitch patterns for steeks

Work the steek stitches in stockinette, using a simple pattern of alternating colors.

163

How to make (and cut) a steek

Work the steek in stockinette, with colors alternating.

Secure it by stitching through the columns on either side of the center stitch.

Then cut through the middle of the center column of stitches. Use sharp scissors!

and sew it into place as a facing or enclose it inside a button band with a facing (see page 113, step 8).

Body knitted back and forth in one piece

This can be a handy technique if you want to avoid side seams and have your body progress evenly, but you don't want to steek. Work as for a circular sweater, with the fronts and the back joined together; however, you will not join to knit in the round. Cast on right front, back, and left front, separating these sections with markers, then turn to work the first row. The beginning and end of the row create the front opening. Make sure your pattern stitches are centered around the front opening (see pages 166–168).

Knit flat with body in one piece, rows ending at center front

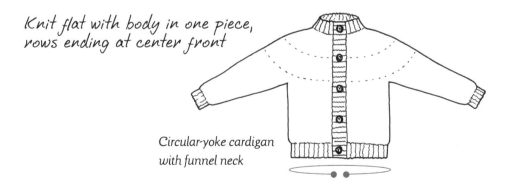

Circular-yoke cardigan with funnel neck

Different ways to make cardigans

Technique	Good for these types of sweaters
In the round with a cut center-front opening	Drop shoulder Square armholes Any sweaters worked in the round with stranded colorwork Sweaters knitted with pure wool yarn or other yarns where the fibers hold together well when cut
Body back and forth in one piece	Raglans Yoke sweater Any sweaters worked in the round knitted with a single color Sweaters knitted with cotton or other slippery yarns
Back and forth in several pieces	Arans Any sweaters with intarsia colorwork Sweaters that do not have manipulations such as cable crossings on wrong-side rows Any sweaters with pattern stitches that have instructions written specifically for flat knitting

Knitting the first and last stitch of every row creates a neat garter-stitch border, which makes it very easy to pick up stitches for the button and buttonhole bands. When you are working with multiple colors, work the first stitch of each row as a locking stitch by working this stitch with every color used in the row.

Back-and-forth bodies for drop-shoulder and square-armhole sweaters

For drop-shoulder and square-armhole sweaters, when you get to the armhole level divide the front and back as for a pullover, except that you have ½ of the total number of stitches in the back and ¼ of the total number of stitches in each of the fronts.

Finish the cardigan back as for a pullover. Then, to finish the cardigan fronts:

☆ For *drop-shoulder sweaters*, work even on each front in the patterns as established until the front measures the desired length to the neck opening.

☆ For *square-shoulder sweaters*, bind off the same number of stitches at the armholes as you did on the back, then work each front in the patterns as established until the front measures the desired length to the neck opening.

Work the neck shaping as for a pullover, binding off ½ of the required stitches on each front at the neck edge and decreasing at the neck edge as for a pullover. For example, if you would bind off 8 stitches at the center for a pullover, bind off 4 stitches on each front.

Even if you don't use a steek for the center-front opening, you can steek the armholes and neck opening, as described in *Ethnic Knitting Discovery*.

Back-and-forth bodies for yoke and raglan sweaters

Remember that if you're doing colorwork, you probably want to be constructing your sweater in the round, not back and forth. See pages 162–164.

For yoke and raglan sweaters, you join the sleeves and the body together as for a pullover, except that you work the yoke back and forth with the opening at the center front. All decreases for shaping are the same as for a pullover.

Knitted back and forth (flat) in several pieces (especially for Arans)

This is a great technique for Aran-style sweaters, because the reverse-side rows usually just knit-the-knits and purl-the-purls and it's easy to remember that cable crossings only happen when you are working a right-side row.

You can't easily convert an Aran pullover sweater into a cardigan. The traditional Aran design has a large cable panel at the center front, and that design can't usually be divided in half to accommodate the opening of a cardigan. Instead, you must design at least the center front portion of an Aran cardigan from scratch.

Most designers center a dominant cable panel on each front section, flanking this panel with smaller cables. Mirror the cables around the center front opening of the cardigan.

Measurements for a cardigan front worked flat in pieces

	Calculation	Example	Description
Body width (whole; same as for pullover)	____ inches (cm)	**20** inches	Measure the **width** of the sweater body.
Front section width	____ ÷ 2 = ____ inches (cm)	20 ÷ 2 = **10** inches	Divide the body width in half for the **width of each front section**.
Neck width (whole)	____ ÷ 3 = ____ inches (cm)	20 ÷ 3 = **6⅔** inches	The **width of the neck** is normally about one-third of the body width. Calculate this or measure your sample sweater.
Front section neck width	____ ÷ 2 = ____ inches (cm)	**3⅓** inches	Divide the width of the whole neck in half to figure out how much of the **neck width** will be on **each front section**.

This table only lists measurements that are different for a cardigan than they are for a pullover. It works for any cardigan that is constructed flat, but I particularly recommend this method for Aran-style garments. See projects 8 and 9 for complete Aran sweater-planning worksheets.

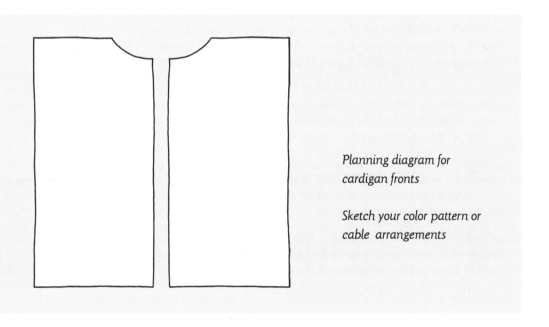

Planning diagram for cardigan fronts

Sketch your color pattern or cable arrangements

After you plot out the cables for the sweater fronts, start from the sides and work toward the center to map a similar set of cables onto the back. Make sure you mirror the cables around the center back to match the arrangement on the fronts so the cables line up at the shoulders.

At the center front of the cardigan, 1 to 1½ inches will be added when you knit the button and buttonhole bands. If you want the back to equal the front in width, add a cable to the center of the back that is approximately equal to the width you are planning for your button bands. This is not required, however. If the back of a sweater is 1 inch (2.5 cm) smaller than the front, it won't make any difference. In fact, adding a little extra ease to a sweater front makes it fit better for women.

After you decide what cables to use and where to place them, verify that this will work by knitting a gauge swatch of all of the cables, as for a pullover (see page 145, step 6).

Calculate the number of stitches you will need for the back and for each of the fronts, based on the number of stitches in each of your cable panels and the side stitches you are planning.

The worksheet at the top of this page provides the extra calculations you'll need for determining the sizes of the front sections and the neck.

Work the back as for the pullover. Work the fronts as for the pullover, except that you will have only half of the number of stitches you had for the back. When you reach the length required to begin neck shaping, end the left front after completing a wrong-side row, and the right front after completing a right-side row.

Work the neck shaping as for a pullover, binding off half of the required stitches on each front at the neck edge and decreasing at the neck edge as for a pullover. For example, if you would bind off 8 stitches at the center for a pullover, bind off 4 stitches on each front. For the right front, the shaping decreases are worked on right-side rows (the beginning of the row). For the left front, the shaping decreases are worked on the wrong-side rows (also at the beginning of the row).

Finishing cardigans

Button and buttonhole bands

If you knitted the sweater body in the round, you can work the front bands before or after you cut the steek.

- ✓ For women's and girls' sweaters, the button band is on the left and the buttonhole band is on the right.

- ✓ For men's and boys' sweaters, the button band is on the right and the buttonhole band is on the left.

Work the button band first. With the right side facing you, pick up stitches along the front edge of the sweater. Use your stitch and row gauge to determine how many stitches to pick up. For example, if your gauge is 3 stitches per inch and 4 rows per inch, pick up 3 stitches for every 4 rows.

Work in ribbing of your choice until the button band is approximately 1 to 1½ inches (2.5 to 3.75 cm) wide. Bind off loosely in pattern.

Work the buttonhole band

Mark positions for the desired number of buttons, placing the first one ½ inch (1.25 cm) from the bottom and the last one ½ inch (1.25 cm) from the top, and spacing the rest evenly between these two.

Work buttonhole band as for button band, making buttonholes when the band is half of the desired width.

Making buttonholes

There are many different ways to make buttonholes. My favorites are described on page 170. If you see another technique elsewhere, give it a try and see if you like it better than these. If you are not sure which type of buttonhole will work with your chosen button, make a small swatch and try several different types of buttonholes to see which comes out the right size for your yarn and buttons.

Yarn-over buttonhole

A simple yarn-over (YO) buttonhole is worked over 2 rows. Although this sounds like it makes a very small buttonhole, I have found that when worked in sport-weight or worsted-weight yarn the opening expands enough to be used with buttons up to 1 inch (2.5 cm) in diameter.

Row 1: When you reach the location for the buttonhole, yarn-over (YO), then work the next 2 stitches together: k2tog if the second stitch is a knit, and p2tog if the second stitch is a purl.

Row 2: When you reach each YO, knit or purl into the YO as necessary to maintain the stitch pattern.

Bind-off buttonhole

The bind-off buttonhole is worked over 3 rows and it makes a larger opening than a yarn-over buttonhole. Be careful, though. If your buttonholes are too big, your sweater won't stay buttoned.

Row 1: When you reach the location for the buttonhole, bind off 2 or 3 stitches.

Row 2: When you reach each buttonhole, cast on the same number of stitches as you bound off in row 1.

Row 3: When you reach each buttonhole, knit or purl into the stitches as necessary to reestablish the stitch pattern.

Neckbands

I like to work the neckband last, so it reaches all the way around the neck and is not interrupted by the front bands. Some designers prefer to work the neckband first so the front bands reach all the way from the top to the bottom of the sweater. The choice is yours.

Pick up stitches around the neck just as for a pullover, but work back and forth, turning at the center-front opening.

If you are working the neckband after the front bands, remember to work one buttonhole on the neckband.

Neckband sequencing options

Option I: Knit neckband first, then front bands.

Option 2: Knit front bands first, then neckband.

Bibliography

Bourgeois, Ann, and Eugene Bourgeois. *Fair Isle Sweaters Simplified.* Bothell, Washington: Martingale & Company, 2000.

Bush, Nancy. *Folk Knitting in Estonia: A Garland of Symbolism, Tradition and Technique.* Loveland, Colorado: Interweave Press, 1999.

Gibson-Roberts, Priscilla A., and Deborah Robson. *Knitting in the Old Way: Designs and Techniques from Ethnic Sweaters.* Fort Collins, Colorado: Nomad Press, 2004.

Guðjónsson, Elsa E. *Notes on Knitting in Iceland.* Reykjavik: [Elsa E. Guðjónsson], 1985.

Knitting around the World from Threads. Newtown, Connecticut: Taunton Press, 1983.

McGregor, Sheila. *The Complete Book of Traditional Scandinavian Knitting.* New York: Saint Martin's Press, 1984.

Merkienė, Irena Regina, and Marija Pautieniūtė-Banionienė. *Lietuvininkų Pirštinės: Kultūrų Kryžkelėje (Gloves of Lithuania Minor: At the Crossroads of Cultures). Lietuvos etnologija* 3. Vilnius, Lithuania: Lietuvos Istorijos Institutas (Institute of Lithuanian History), 1998.

Sundbø, Annemor. *Setesdal Sweaters: The History of the Norwegian Lice Pattern.* Kristiansand, Norway: Torridal Tweed, 2001.

Starmore, Alice. *Aran Knitting.* Loveland, Colorado: Interweave Press, 1997.

Swansen, Meg. *Meg Swansen's Knitting.* Loveland, Colorado: Interweave Press, 1999.

Zimmermann, Elizabeth. *The Opinionated Knitter.* Pittsville, Wisconsin: Schoolhouse Press, 2005.

Translating from fractions to decimals for ease of calculator use

$\frac{1}{8} = .125$ $\frac{3}{8} = .375$ $\frac{5}{8} = .625$ $\frac{7}{8} = .875$

$\frac{1}{4} = .25$ $\frac{1}{2} = .5$ $\frac{3}{4} = .75$

Index

Acknowledgments

Reading through the final proof of this book, I was surprised by how much I like it. I always forget my books between when I write them and when I get them back from my publisher, all dolled-up with gorgeous pictures and with the text improved by expert editing. Sometimes I like them much more than I remembered. That's how I feel about *Ethnic Knitting Exploration.*

Special thanks goes to all of the people who made this book better than it was when I turned in the manuscript: to Deb Robson, editor *extraordinaire* (she should actually be listed as co-author of this book), who also created charts and schematics and yet more swatches and also took photos and made the layout happen; to Joyce M. Turley for turning my sketches into beautiful fashion illustrations; to Rebekah Robson-May for making all of the pictures the best quality possible for printing; to Debbie O'Neill for designing and knitting the cover sweaters; to JoAnne Turcotte and Plymouth Yarn Co. for the yarn used to knit the cover sweaters; to Joyce Druchunas for knitting vast quantities of swatches and for always telling me how creative I am; to Monica Thomas of TLCGraphics for designing such a wonderful cover; and to Katie Banks, for her Eagle-Eye indexing and proofreading.

And thank you for reading this book. I hope it encourages you to make your own explorations into the world of ethnic knitting.

Colophon

Text fonts are Warnock Pro (Robert Slimbach; Adobe), Myriad Pro (Robert Slimbach and Carol Twombly, with Fred Brady and Christopher Slye; Adobe), and Rodeo Girl BV (Jess Latham; Blue Vinyl Fonts). Display fonts and dingbats are Abbey Road NF (Nick Curtis; Nick's Fonts), LTC Goudy Sans (Fredric Goudy, with supplements by Colin Kahn; Lanston Type Company/P22), Arrows (The FontSite), Dingbats, FF Dingbests (Johannes Erler and Olaf Stein; FontFont), P22 Tulda (Frau Jenson; P22), TF Neue Neuland Ornaments (Joseph Treacy; Treacy Faces), LTC Vine Leaves (Lanston Type Company/P22), and Adobe Wood Type Ornaments (Barbara Lind and Joy Redick; Adobe).

Nomad Press is a member of the Green Press Initiative and a signatory of the Book Industry Treatise on Responsible Paper Use (www.greenpressinitiative.org).